W9-AUY-027

Maya Angelou

Published in the United States of America by Cherry Lake Publishing
Ann Arbor, Michigan
www.cherrylakepublishing.com

Content Adviser: Ryan Emery Hughes, Doctoral Student, School of Education, University of Michigan
Reading Adviser: Marla Conn MS, Ed., Literacy specialist, Read-Ability, Inc.
Book Design: Jennifer Wahi
Illustrator: Jeff Bane

Photo Credits: © Colin Stitt/Shutterstock, 5; © B Christopher / Alamy Stock Photo, 7; © Everett Collection Historical / Alamy Stock Photo, 9; © Warren K. Leffler/Library of Congress, 11; © Ambient Ideas/Shutterstock, 13, 22; © Jack Sotomayor / Contributor/Getty, 15; © The Washington Post / Contributor, 17; © Courtesy, William J. Clinton Presidential Library/Wikimedia, 19, 23; © Adrian Sherratt / Alamy Stock Photo, 21; Cover, 8, 14, 18, Jeff Bane; Various frames throughout, Shutterstock Images

Library of Congress Cataloging-in-Publication Data

Names: Haldy, Emma E., author. | Bane, Jeff, 1957- illustrator.
Title: Maya Angelou / Emma E. Haldy ; [illustrated by Jeff Bane].
Description: Ann Arbor : Cherry Lake Publishing, 2017. | Series: My
   itty-bitty bio | Includes bibliographical references and index.
Identifiers: LCCN 2016031796| ISBN 9781634721530 (hardcover) | ISBN
   9781634722858 (pbk.) | ISBN 9781634722193 (pdf) | ISBN 9781634723510
   (ebook)
Subjects: LCSH: Angelou, Maya--Juvenile literature. | African American women
   authors--Biography--Juvenile literature. | Authors, American--20th
   century--Biography--Juvenile literature.
Classification: LCC PS3551.N464 Z684 2017 | DDC 818/.5409 [B] --dc23
LC record available at https://lccn.loc.gov/2016031796

Printed in the United States of America
Corporate Graphics

table of contents

About the author: Emma E. Haldy is a former librarian and a proud Michigander. She lives with her husband, Joe, and an ever-growing collection of books.

About the illustrator: Jeff Bane and his two business partners own a studio along the American River in Folsom, California, home of the 1849 Gold Rush. When Jeff's not sketching or illustrating for clients, he's either swimming or kayaking in the river to relax.

I was born in 1928. I had one brother.

My grandma raised us. We lived in Arkansas.

My family was black. We were treated unfairly.

My childhood was not easy.

What would it feel like to be treated unfairly?

Books helped me feel better.
I loved to read.

I also loved to sing and dance.
I became a **performer**.

America was changing. I was a part of it.

I wanted all people to be treated fairly.

I enjoyed writing. I decided to write a book.

It was about my childhood. It was about being black.

Would you like to write a book?
Why or why not?

The book was special. It gave people a new **perspective**.

It was a **best seller**. I won awards.

I was famous. I wrote more books. I wrote plays. I wrote poetry.

I was a voice for my community.

I read a poem when Bill Clinton became president.

It was a beautiful moment! I was happy to be an American.

I was honored for many years.
I kept writing until my death.

I was an **inspirational** woman.
I wrote. I performed. I told stories
through art.

What would you like to ask me?

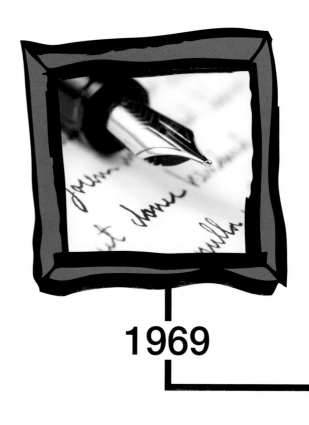

1969

1930

Born
1928

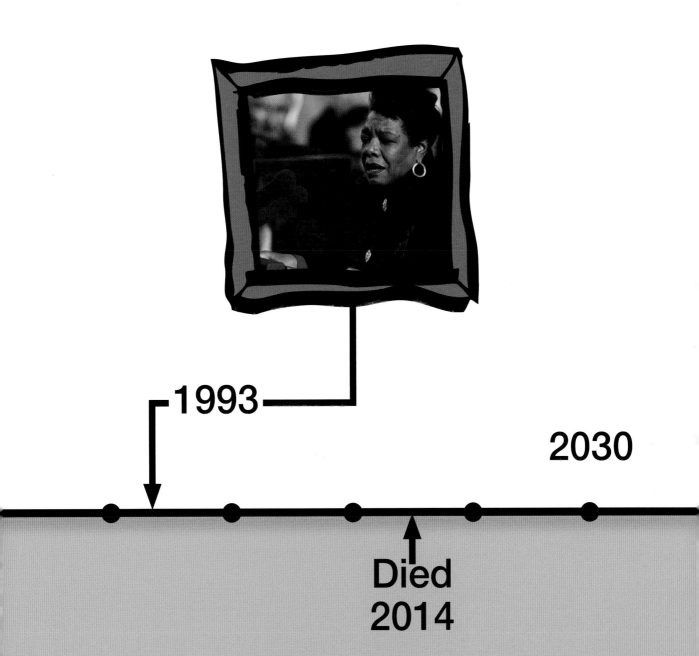

1993

2030

Died
2014

glossary

best seller (best SEL-ur) a popular book that many people have bought

inspirational (in-spuh-RAY-shuh-nuhl) filling someone with an emotion, an idea, or an attitude

performer (pur-FOR-mur) a person who reads, sings, dances, or acts in front of others in public

perspective (pur-SPEK-tiv) a certain way of looking at something

index

The Quest for Freedom:
The Abolitionist Movement

Lucent Library of Black History

Stephen Currie

LUCENT BOOKS

An imprint of Thomson Gale, a part of The Thomson Corporation

Detroit • New York • San Francisco • San Diego • New Haven, Conn.
Waterville, Maine • London • Munich

LIBRARY OF CONGRESS CATALOGING-IN-PUBLICATION DATA

Currie, Stephen, 1960-
    The quest for freedom : the abolitionist movement / by Stephen Currie.
        p. cm. -- (Lucent library of Black history)
    Includes bibliographical references and index.
    ISBN 1-59018-703-2 (alk. paper)
    1. United States—History—Juvenile literature. 2. Slavery—United States—History—
Juvenile literature. I. Title. II. Series.
E441.C86 2005
973.7'114—dc22

2005006304

Printed in the United States of America

Contents

Foreword

It has been more than five hundred years since Africans were first brought to the New World in shackles, and over 140 years since slavery was formally abolished in the United States. Over 50 years have passed since the fallacy of "separate but equal" was obliterated in the American courts, and some forty years since the watershed Civil Rights Act of 1965 guaranteed the rights and liberties of all Americans, especially those of color. Over time, these changes have become celebrated landmarks in American history. In the twenty-first century, African American men and women are politicians, judges, diplomats, professors, deans, doctors, artists, athletes, business owners, and home owners. For many, the scars of the past have melted away in the opportunities that have been found in contemporary society. Observers such as Peter N. Kirsanow, who sits on the U.S. Commission of Civil Rights, point to these accomplishments and conclude, "The growing black middle class may be viewed as proof that most of the civil rights battles have been won."

In spite of these legal victories, however, prejudice and inequality have persisted in American society. In 2003, African Americans comprised just 12 percent of the nation's population, yet accounted for 44 percent of its prison inmates and 24 percent of its poor. Racially motivated hate crimes continue to appear on the pages of major newspapers in many American cities. Furthermore, many African Americans still experience either overt or muted racism in their daily lives. A 1996 study undertaken by Professor Nancy Krieger of the Harvard School of Public Health, for example, found that 80 percent of the African American participants reported having experienced racial discrimination in one or more settings, including at work or school, applying for housing and medical care, from the police or in the courts, and on the street or in a public setting.

It is for these reasons that many believe the struggle for racial equality and justice is far from over. These episodes of discrimination threaten to shatter the illusion that America has completely overcome its racist past, causing many black Americans to become increasingly frustrated and confused. Scholar and writer Ellis Cose has described this splintered state in the following way: "I have done everything I was supposed to do. I have stayed out of trouble with the law, gone to the right schools, and worked myself nearly to death. What more do they want? Why in God's name won't they accept me as a full human being?" For Cose and others, the struggle for equality and justice has yet to be fully achieved.

In many subtle yet important ways the traumatic experiences of slavery and segregation continue to inform the way race is discussed and experienced in the twenty-first century. Indeed, it is possible that America will always grapple with the fallout from its distressing past. Ulric Haynes, dean of the Hofstra University School of Business has said, "Perhaps race will always matter, given the historical circumstances under which we came to this country." But studying this past and understanding how it contributes to present-day dialogues about race and history in America is a critical component of contemporary education. To this end, the Lucent Library of Black History offers a thorough look at the experiences that have shaped the black community and the American people as a whole. Annotated bibliographies provide readers with ideas for further research, while fully documented primary and secondary source quotations enhance the text. Each book in the series explores a different episode of black history; together they provide students with a wealth of information as well as launching points for further study and discussion.

Introduction

The Abolitionists

Just before 1830, a newly organized group of social reformers began to agitate for change in the United States. Their goal was to eliminate, or abolish, the institution of slavery within the United States; for that reason, these reformers were widely known as the abolitionists. Over the next three decades and more, these activists worked tirelessly for their cause. Angry, determined, and absolutely certain that they were in the right, the men and women who joined the abolitionist movement helped to change the course of American history.

The abolitionists were a varied and often uneasy mix of personalities and perspectives. The movement encompassed white and black, male and female, rich and poor. The activists included evangelical preachers from the Midwest side by side with newspaper editors from New England, daughters of Southern planters together with blacks who had escaped from slavery. Some were self-proclaimed radicals who wanted to destroy slavery as quickly as possible, whatever the consequences; others were moderates who preferred to dismantle the institution slowly and carefully. Only one feature, in the end, linked the abolitionists to each other: their shared abhorrence of slavery.

Like most reform movements, the abolition movement was extremely controversial during most of its existence. It was scorned, even hated, by a large percentage of the American population, and it was viewed with deep suspicion by many more.

Critics complained that the reformers were irresponsible, overzealous, and misguided. Even sympathetic audiences often thought that the abolitionists went too far. Supporters of the movement frequently encouraged the abolitionists to tone down their rhetoric, restrain their attacks, and do more to understand their opponents. "Do try to moderate your indignation, and keep more cool," one man counseled abolitionist newspaper editor William Lloyd Garrison; "why, you are all on fire."[1]

To the abolitionists, though, moderating their indignation was neither desirable nor possible. In their minds, they were battling an institution that was morally bankrupt, spiritually unsound, and sinful in the extreme. They viewed slavery as brutal, violent, and dehumanizing, and they had evidence to prove their point. "Must I argue that a system thus marked with blood, and stained with pollution, is wrong?"[2] demanded Frederick Douglass, an escaped slave turned abolitionist. As activists like Douglass and Garrison saw it, keeping silent in the face of such evil was simply not an option.

The Institution of Slavery

It can be difficult for modern audiences to understand why the abolitionists encountered such a negative reaction. Slavery is dead in modern America, of course, and support for slavery is nonexistent. In the twenty-first century, the idea of holding innocent people in bondage and forcing them to perform unpaid labor is seen as repugnant. Slavery is remembered today, therefore, as an embarrassing relic of the American past, an appalling and inexcusable breach of the rights of ordinary people. Given these views, there appears to be no reason why anyone would ever have supported the institution.

But the twenty-first century is not the nineteenth century. During the 1800s, America was a different place, with different traditions and different standards. There were reasons why slavery arose in the British colonies to begin with, reasons why it lasted—at least in the American South—and reasons why millions of otherwise moral and ethical Americans objected to the abolitionists' message. The abolitionists of the 1830s and beyond were attacking an institution that had many, many defenders, an institution that was accepted and appreciated by a large segment of

Slave women sow rice on a North Carolina plantation in this illustration. Until the end of the Civil War in 1865, slavery was a firmly entrenched institution in the South.

the population—and an institution that, by any standard, was flourishing where it existed.

Nevertheless, even before 1830, when the abolitionist movement formed, slavery was already controversial, and some Americans had raised objections to the institution. Indeed, American slavery presented deep contradictions. By 1830, it was essential to the economic well-being of the South—and yet, at the same time, it was forbidden across virtually the entire North. The United States, Americans liked to proclaim, had been founded to ensure the freedom of its people—and yet it denied freedom altogether to millions of slaves. In the end, the contradictions of slavery became impossible to resolve quickly and easily. As historian Bruce Catton writes, slavery proved to be "the issue that could not be compromised, the issue that made men so angry they did not want to compromise."[3]

The abolitionists of the period 1830–1865 helped make it difficult to compromise on slavery. They took earlier objections to slavery, reworked them, and added new ones. Their ability to organize, their single-minded determination to destroy the slave system, and their unwillingness to compromise made them a powerful force indeed. Though they did not always accomplish exactly what they hoped to achieve, the efforts of the abolitionists succeeded in changing the way Americans thought about slavery—and their efforts were invaluable in bringing an end to the institution. Principled, courageous, and above all resolute, the abolitionists had an impact that cannot be denied.

Chapter One

Slavery in America

The men and women who made up the abolitionist movement were fighting against an abusive and dehumanizing system: the institution of slavery. As these activists saw it, slavery oppressed and brutalized African Americans, corrupted Southern slaveholders, and disgraced the entire American nation. The abolitionists' revulsion toward slavery led them to risk their reputations, their careers, and sometimes their lives to oppose what they saw as a great moral wrong. Slavery gave the abolitionists both their name and their cause. In order to understand the abolitionist movement, it is first necessary to understand slavery.

Slaves as Property

American slavery began to take shape during the mid-1600s. At first, the institution grew slowly and somewhat haphazardly. By 1700, there were only about twenty-eight thousand slaves scattered across Britain's North American colonies. But as the century progressed, slavery became more and more profitable—and more and more common. In 1750, there were more than a quarter million slaves in America; fifty years later, the slave population stood at nearly nine hundred thousand, most of them involved in agriculture and nearly all of them living in the Southern states. As the United States expanded westward and new, more effective farming methods came into use, the number of slaves continued to increase. In 1860, about two hundred years after the beginning of the institution on American soil, about four million slaves lived and labored in the United States.

Throughout its history, the fundamental truth—and the fundamental tragedy—of American slavery had to do with the legal status of the slave. American slaves, like American slaveholders, were human beings. They were mothers and fathers, daughters and sons; they were people with thoughts and feelings, hopes and fears, wishes and dreams. Yet under the laws of the slave states, American slaves were not considered fully human. Instead, they were property, viewed little differently from cattle or land. "A slave by our code is not treated as a person," a Kentucky court admitted in 1828, "but a thing."[4]

To be sure, slaves were not consistently classed as objects. Although the laws of the slave states generally considered slaves to be property, legal scholars knew perfectly well that slaves were fundamentally unlike tools, houses, or animals. A plow, after all, could not plan an escape from its owner, nor could a wagon refuse to work or a sheep organize an armed rebellion; but a slave could do all three. "[Slaves] have wills of their own," explained a South Carolina judge, "[and] capacities to commit crimes; and are responsible for offences against society."[5] Thus, slaves who escaped, who were caught out of their dwellings after curfew, or

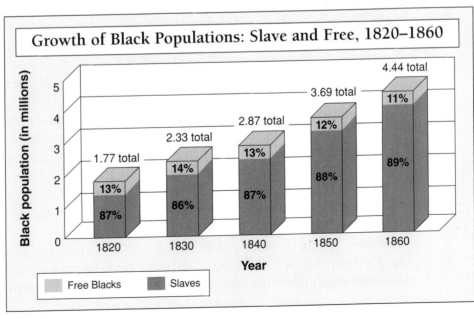

Growth of Black Populations: Slave and Free, 1820–1860

who struck their masters were acting not as property, but as human beings, and for this reason, they could be punished to the full extent of the law.

However, American legal codes recognized the slaves' humanity only where punishment was concerned. It made no sense to talk of the rights of hammers and horses, slaveholders argued, and so it made no sense to talk of the rights of slaves. Throughout the slave states, as a result, laws did very little to protect slaves from mistreatment. Masters could beat, torture, or even kill their slaves, and unless the circumstances of the case were especially appalling, the judicial system would not intervene, any more than it would intervene if farmers destroyed their barns or damaged their fences. As one early Virginia law put it, in the event that a master killed one of his or her slaves, "the master shall be free of all punishment . . . as if such accident never happened."[6]

Race, Permanence, and Heredity

Besides equating slaves with property, the institution of American slavery rested on three important principles. The first involved race. Other than a brief attempt to enslave Indians early in colonial history, colonial laws held that African Americans—and only African Americans—could be kept in bondage. Though not all black Americans who lived before 1860 were slaves, the great majority of them were. And all American slaves either came directly from Africa or were of African descent.

But slavery was not just racial; it was permanent, as well. Once enslaved, slaves remained in that condition until they died. There was no set number of years after which slaves could demand their liberty, no task a slave could perform that would guarantee his or her release from bondage. True, masters occasionally chose to free their slaves or allowed some of their slaves to purchase their freedom. However, these actions were rare, and the decision was the master's, not the slave's. For the vast majority of slaves, the sad reality was that slavery was forever.

Worse, American slavery was hereditary. The children of a slave were automatically classed as slaves themselves. So were the slave's grandchildren; so, for that matter, were all the future descendants of a slave. As an early Maryland law expressed it, "All children now born [of slaves], or hereafter to be born . . . shall be slaves during their natural lives."[7] In the American system, then, there was no easy way out of bondage—either for individual slaves, or for the generations yet to come.

Along with the view that slaves were property, the characteristics of race, permanence, and heredity defined American slavery. Together, they created two separate and sharply unequal classes of people: free whites and black slaves. Both by law and by custom, rights and privileges belonged exclusively to the free people of the region. With very few exceptions, the slaves had no rights that any free person was required to respect. The system stripped the slave of every vestige of humanity. It denied, in effect, that slaves were truly people.

An overseer looks on as one slave is forced to whip another in front of the other slaves on the plantation. Slaves were routinely subject to extremely harsh corporal punishment.

Brutality and Violence

Under these circumstances, slavery, as practiced in the agricultural South during the nineteenth century, was brutal and oppressive. While a minority of slaveholders seldom, if ever, lifted a hand against a slave, most slaves found violence an inescapable part of their lives. On Southern plantations—large farms on which cotton, rice, and other important crops were grown—slaves were frequently subjected to beatings, whippings, and other physical punishments. The effects of the punishment were long-lasting. As former slave Mary Reynolds told an interviewer seventy years after the end of the Civil War, "I got the scars on my old body to show to this day."[8]

A shirtless slave stands tied to a whipping post as his master prepares to flog him.

Most slaves who received physical punishment were beaten for a specific offense. These offenses ranged from the serious to the trivial. A slave could be beaten for refusing to work—or for being the last one into the fields one morning, even if only by a matter of seconds. A slave could be whipped for working too slowly, for taking an item belonging to the master, for speaking to a white person in a way that could be interpreted as disrespectful. Because all authority belonged to the master, the master decided what would be a punishable offense.

Whatever the offense, there was general agreement among Southern slaveholders that physical punishment was necessary. Most masters believed that only a fool would try to control slaves through gentle means, such as using verbal encouragement or promising rewards for good behavior. Instead, slaveholders argued, slaves responded only to the threat of the whip and the pain of a beating. "He must be *made* to work," insisted an Arkansas planter, speaking of the typical slave, "and should always be given to understand that if he fails to perform his duty he will be punished for it."[9]

Whippings and Other Punishments

Whippings were the most common physical punishment that slaves experienced. Usually, slaves who were whipped were stripped at least to the waist; then they were made to bend over or lie down to receive their punishment. Most punishments consisted of ten or twenty lashes, but some slaves were subjected to repeated blows that far exceeded these limits. At these levels, the beatings had the potential to kill. "They took him and whupped him for near fifteen minutes," recalled one former slave about a fieldhand subjected to a particularly brutal punishment for taking money from his master. "He never got over that whupping. He died three days later."[10]

Even a beating of no more than a dozen strokes could be devastating to both body and spirit. Whips used by the slaveholders were long and thick, with hooks and lashes designed to cut into the flesh of the victim, and the backs of many slaves bore silent testimony to the damage caused by repeated lashings. The psychic scars, moreover, could be even worse than the physical. "I lays in de bunk two days, gittin' over dat whippin'," recalled Texas slave Andy Marion about a particularly brutal beating; "gittin' over it in de body but not in de heart. No, suh, I has dat in de heart till dis day."[11]

Whippings were not the only punishment given to slaves. Nor, for all the pain they caused, were they necessarily the worst. Slaves were shackled all day to posts in the hot sun, forced to eat worms, or held in solitary confinement. Some were branded. Recaptured runaway slaves, in particular, were often punished by having iron rings, weights, and chains attached to their legs, their arms, or even their necks. Many masters refused to use these painful and humiliating punishments. Still, the law offered slaves no protection from owners who sometimes seemed eager to inflict pain in the most appalling way possible.

Usually, the punishments given to slaves were ineffective. Even slaves who carried chains on their legs and necks still tried to run away from their owners. Southern newspapers frequently included advertisements seeking the return of slaves who had vanished into the woods regardless of their chains. "Ranaway," read one such notice from Mississippi, "a black woman, Betsey—had an iron bar on her right leg."[12] And given that most slaves were beaten repeatedly, it was evident that whipping was hardly an effective means of "reforming" them; if it had been, then one punishment would have sufficed.

The punishments, however, were not generally designed to correct bad behavior. They were intended, instead, to terrify and to humiliate. To the planters, it was imperative that slaves recognize the authority of the masters, and there was no better way of getting that message across than through the use of physical punishment. The possibility of being beaten, for any reason or, occasionally, for no reason at all, was constantly on the mind of nearly every slave, and that was just as the slaveholders desired. In a letter to a friend, a North Carolina slave owner neatly expressed the central purpose of the brutality that marked American slavery. It was, she remarked, "to make [the slaves] stand in fear."[13]

"They Work Both Night and Day"

Physical punishment was not the only means by which masters routinely asserted their authority over their slaves. Overwork was another. In the agrarian South, slaves labored hard, and they labored long. Most slaves had Sundays off, and many were given parts of Saturdays for leisure, but on the other days of the week, slaves spent the vast majority of their waking hours working.

Agricultural slaves began their labors early—often, before dawn. Some masters offered their slaves a midday rest break when the temperature reached its hottest, but others drove the slaves to continue without a pause. "He never let us eat at noon," former slave Ben Simpson said of his master; "he worked us all day without stopping."[14] At dusk, the slaves were usually permitted to quit for the day; but when the need was great, such as during harvest time, they were sometimes kept at work well past

"He Is *Not* a Slave"

———■———

There were many similarities between the lives of the slaves and the lives of the peasants of Europe or the factory workers of the North. Slaveholders sometimes pointed to these similarities to justify their institution. Those who opposed slavery were usually forced to admit that the peasants and ordinary laborers of free societies were not well-treated, either. However, the peasants and laborers had one great advantage. Escaped slave turned reformer Frederick Douglass addressed the specific claim that Irish peasants were no better off than slaves where material goods were concerned in an 1850 lecture, quoted in Philip S. Foner, ed., *Frederick Douglass: Selected Speeches and Writings:* "There is no analogy between the two cases. The Irishman is poor, but he is *not* a slave. He *may* be in rags, but he is *not* a slave. He is still the master of his own body." It was an important distinction, and one the abolitionist movement would emphasize again and again.

sunset. "The night was shortened at both ends,"[15] lamented slave-turned-abolitionist Frederick Douglass.

The long hours might not have been so bad had the tasks been easier. But the work of a typical slave was difficult, repetitive, and often painful. Picking cotton, for instance, required constant bending and stooping, and thorns on the cotton plants pierced the fingers of even the most careful harvesters. Rice was grown in swampy areas that were home to snakes, mosquitoes, and maggots. For nearly all slaves, performing such work for ten or twelve hours was torture enough. To labor under these conditions for sixteen or eighteen hours pushed most slaves to the absolute limits of their endurance.

Living Conditions

The basics of life—food, clothing, and shelter—were another way in which slaves suffered. By custom, and in a few cases by law, these necessities were to be provided by the slaveholders. Some plantation owners did offer their slaves a nutritious diet, sturdy housing, and clothing appropriate for the season. Unfortunately, many others did not. Even given the standards of the nineteenth century, the food, clothing, and housing afforded to many American slaves were simply inadequate.

For many slaves, food was a key problem. The list of slave complaints regarding food usually began with the amount offered by the slaveholders. Though few slaves starved, many—perhaps most—were constantly hungry. Thoughtful masters, recognizing that a well-fed slave could do more work than one weakened by hunger, did not stint on the quantity of food they allowed their slaves. But other masters saw no need to spend money on extra rations. "They never was as much [food] as we needed,"[16] mourned Mary Reynolds.

The selection and content of the food was a problem as well. Few nineteenth-century Americans, slave or free, ate what would be considered a nutritionally balanced diet today. Still, too many slaveholders fed their charges a dull, unvarying menu of foods that provided little in the way of vitamins and nutrients. Some masters, for instance, gave their slaves virtually nothing but cornmeal. Those who offered their workers other foods often economized by providing fare that was fatty or spoiled. "The pork was often tainted," recalled Frederick Douglass of his years in slavery, "and the fish were of the poorest quality."[17]

Just as slave food was usually substandard, so too was housing. On large plantations, slaves lived in the "quarters"—a small group of shacks set aside strictly for the use of the slaves. A few masters insisted that the slave quarters be reasonably clean and comfortable. However, most did not. Throughout the South, slaves lived in cramped, dingy wooden huts, with earthen floors and empty spaces where windowpanes should have been. One former slave, Solomon Northup, remembered using a narrow wooden board for a bed. "The bedding," he added, "was a coarse blanket, and not a rag or shred beside."[18]

Clothing was no better. Not all masters made hats or shoes available to their slaves. "I have known slaves who went without shoes all winter," reported a Virginia man. "The feet of many of them are frozen."[19] Slave clothes were typically made from coarse, itchy fabrics, which were not merely uncomfortable but which tore and ripped easily as well. Slave owners were slow to substitute damaged clothing with new outfits, perhaps because they feared that doing so would encourage slaves to destroy their old garments in hopes of getting replacements. As a result, slaves frequently wore nothing but rags.

Separation

The life of a slave was filled with adversity. Slaves complained bitterly—and legitimately—about overwork, punishment, and living conditions. But for most slaves, what made slavery most unbearable had nothing to do with whippings, substandard housing, or even a twenty-hour stint in the fields. Instead, what frightened slaves the most was the prospect of being sold away from their families and friends.

Masters had absolute authority over their slaves, and among those powers was the ability to sell any slave, at any time, for any reason. Hundreds of thousands of slaves were sold at some point

A slave family is up for auction in this 1852 painting. Slaves lived in constant fear of being separated from family and friends.

Resistance and Rebellion

■

Few slaves dared to resist their masters openly. The consequences of doing so were simply too dangerous. A slave who actually talked back in anger, let alone struck back, was risking his or her life. "I never had a whopping and you can't whop me," one slave told his master. "But I can kill you," the master replied; and taking out a gun, he did exactly that. Stories such as this one, from B.A. Botkin, ed., *Lay My Burden Down*, are easy to find in any anthology of slave narratives.

Still, slaves did resist their masters in other ways. Many ran away, whether planning a dash north for freedom or simply running off into the forest to avoid a beating or an excessive workload. In some wilderness areas, whole communities of slaves formed, scavenging for food, setting up makeshift tents, and keeping away from their masters for weeks or even months. The life was difficult, but for many slaves it was preferable to life under the control of the master.

Slaves also fought back by doing less work than they were supposed to do. Some cotton pickers, assigned to collect a certain weight of cotton, put rocks at the bottom of their baskets. Slaves occasionally pretended to have forgotten how to use a plow, identify weeds, or clean a carpet, forcing their masters to "teach" them what they already knew; this gave the slaves a rest break and had the added advantage of infuriating their masters. And when they were not being carefully monitored, slaves often reduced their working pace to a crawl. In all these ways, slaves fought back against an unjust system.

during their lives, some to a neighboring planter, but others to farmers who lived several states away. These sales often resulted in the separation of families. The reminiscences of former slaves who were separated by sale are some of the saddest in all the annals of slavery. "I seized hold of her hand, while my mind felt unutterable things," recalled Virginia slave Henry Brown of the day when his wife, Nancy, was sold away from him. "Both our hearts were so overpowered with feeling that we could say nothing."[20]

Defenders of slavery conceded that family members were

occasionally separated through sale. They insisted, however, that the practice was extremely rare. Certainly, many slaveholders refused on principle to engage in such a transaction. But hundreds, perhaps thousands, of Southern planters had no such scruples. Whether in hopes of earning a bigger profit or in an attempt to make up for financial losses, they readily sold husbands away from their wives, mothers from their children, children from their brothers and sisters.

The breaking up of families through sale may have been the most appalling result of slavery. But it was not the only way in which slaves were reminded that they could never be in charge of their own lives and their own fates. Slaves could not escape the threat of punishment, could not escape the fear of sale, could not even provide themselves with a sturdy pair of shoes—and certainly could not lift themselves to freedom. Each day, in ways great and small, slaves were reminded that they had no voice, no rights—and, in essence, no humanity. That, in the end, was what made slavery such an unspeakable tragedy.

Chapter Two

Colonial Abolitionists

Most historians consider the American abolitionist movement to date from about 1830, when antislavery thinkers across the North banded together in passionate opposition to the slave system. But long before the formation of this movement, a few Americans were already voicing their objections to slavery. These early thinkers did not have the impact of the later activists; they did not organize themselves as their successors did, nor did they use the same range of strategies to attack the slave system. Nonetheless, their ideas served as a foundation for the stronger, more adamant movement that lay ahead. The work of the antislavery reformers of colonial America and the Revolutionary period paved the way for the abolitionists of the 1830s and beyond.

Origins of American Slavery

By 1670, with little or no debate, slavery had been written into the laws of every existing British colony. In part, the colonists were inspired to institute slavery by the example of their neighbors in South America and the Caribbean. By the early 1500s, various European powers had established farms, mines, and factories in these parts of the New World and were importing thousands of Africans a year to serve as forced laborers. Though slavery in places like Cuba and Brazil was appallingly brutal, there was no denying the economic success enjoyed by the Europeans on whose behalf the slaves toiled. It made sense to the British colonists in Virginia, Massachusetts, and elsewhere to adopt the same formula themselves.

Noah, Ham, and Canaan

The biblical account of Noah's ark and the great flood, found in the book of Genesis, closes with a scene in which Noah becomes deeply offended by the actions of his youngest son, Ham. To punish Ham for his misdeeds, Noah lays a curse on Ham's son Canaan. "Accursed be Canaan," reads Genesis 9:25, "He shall be his brothers' meanest slave." The curse, however, did not affect only Canaan; it also affected all of Canaan's descendants through the rest of time.

The defenders of slavery used this story to support their view that slavery was acceptable in the Bible, but they added an extra twist. Although the Bible never says so specifically, it was a long tradition among European Christians that all Africans were descended from Ham and Canaan, while Europeans and Asians were descended from Noah's other sons. Under this reasoning, slavery was not only justifiable, it had been specifically designed for Africans. Indeed, through Noah, it seemed that God had ordained that African people should serve the people of Europe. This connection strengthened the view of Europeans that the enslavement of blacks in particular was acceptable and morally sound.

Proponents of slavery believed that all slaves were descended from the cursed grandson of Noah (pictured with his family after the Flood).

Slavery, too, seemed to be justified by history and religion. The ancient Greeks, the early Romans, the Muslims of the medieval Middle East—all had owned slaves, a fact known to the early colonists. These and other societies, moreover, had been powerful, productive civilizations. Many observers believed there was a direct connection between the existence of slavery and the rise of these great cultures. By this reasoning, instituting slavery seemed likely to help the colonists achieve great things.

In the view of Europeans, the Bible, too, not only accepted but ordained slavery. That was particularly true of the Old Testament: Leviticus 25:44–46, for instance, instructed the ancient Hebrews to buy servants of other cultures and to hold them in bondage forever. The New Testament, in turn, had fewer references to slavery, but never specifically said that slavery was not acceptable. European Christians of the 1600s saw the Bible as the literal word of God, and if God had justified slavery, it was not their place to question the institution.

More generally, to the white colonists of the 1600s, slavery was an unremarkable part of life. In the European worldview, the existence of social classes was natural and divinely ordained. "God . . . hath Ordained different degrees and orders of men," wrote colonial Massachusetts judge John Saffin, "some to be High and Honourable, some to be Low and Despicable; some to be Monarchs, Kings, Princes, and Governours . . . others to be Subjects, and to be Commanded."[21] Slaves, in this view, were simply the lowest of the low—the people who appeared at the very bottom of this social order.

The existence of slavery was even easier for Europeans to accept because Africans were of a different race. In the 1400s and 1500s, European explorers had begun traveling to West Africa, thus initiating the first serious contacts between black Africans and white Europeans. Most of the European adventurers were unimpressed, even repulsed, by the peoples they encountered. From the explorers' perspective, the Africans were violent, unclean, and immoral. (The Africans, it should be noted, had many of the same reactions to the European explorers.) Europeans quickly came to believe that Africans were an inferior race that could—and should—be enslaved.

In instituting slavery, then, the North American colonists were acting as creatures of their time. The colonists never doubted the morality of their actions. The colonists, after all, had been born into a world that believed slavery was divinely ordained; that championed the superiority of whites over blacks; that accepted slavery's role in creating great and wealthy civilizations. It was easy, then, for the British settlers to adopt the system of slavery without any concern about its morality or its impact on the Africans they enslaved.

The Quakers

But in the late 1600s, opposition to American slavery began to grow. Among the first Americans to voice concerns about slavery were members of the Society of Friends, a religious group more commonly known as the Quakers. The Quakers' ideas about religion made them distinct in colonial America—and in England, where the sect had originated in the mid-1600s. Unlike members of the mainstream, established Church of England, for example, Quakers worshipped in simple, spare spaces, and their services typically included no music, statements of beliefs, or rituals.

There was a social and political component to Quaker thought, too. In sharp contrast to the sentiments that prevailed throughout England and the colonies during the 1600s, Quaker teachings held that all people were fundamentally equal. Quakers hired no priests or other ministers to lead services, believing instead that all worshippers could, and should, have direct access to the divine. Indeed, according to Quaker principles, all people carried within them an element of God's spirit. As John 1:9 put it, "The true Light [of God] . . . lighteth every man that cometh into the world."

This notion of equality, of course, called into question several basic assumptions that ordinary Europeans—and ordinary American colonists—made about the world around them. It led Quakers to question the right of kings to rule and the need for priests to interpret the word of God for others. It also led them to champion the rights of the oppressed, a list that included women, the poor, and, in particular, slaves. According to Quakers, if all people carried the light of the Gospel in their souls, then slaves deserved the same rights as free people, and slavery was an unjust and terrible institution.

A large congregation of Quakers attends a meeting in this eighteenth-century illustration. Quakers were among the first American abolitionists.

To be sure, not all Quakers believed in the equality of all people. Quakerism had no official doctrines and no church hierarchy. There was no way to ensure that all members accepted the same teachings on slavery, and indeed many did not. Some Quakers owned slaves or bought and sold them as part of their business. Others played no part in slavery, but had no objection if neighbors or family members chose to have slaves of their own. Still, many of the Quakers who immigrated to the North American colonies were strongly antislavery. These thinkers were among the first American abolitionists.

"The Colour of a Man Avails Nothing"

The first important antislavery statement in America was issued in 1688, when some Friends in Germantown, Pennsylvania, publicly expressed their opinion that slavery was a great evil. Their argument rested in large part on ethical and philosophical foundations. Slavery, these Quakers argued, represented the theft of

John Woolman

◾

Of the eighteenth-century Quakers who disapproved of slavery, John Woolman, a shopkeeper and scribe who lived and worked in New Jersey, may be the most famous today. Woolman's journey to abolitionism was long, complex, and extremely personal. As a shopkeeper and a scribe, Woolman did not own slaves himself and took pride in that reality. As he thought more about the subject, however, he realized that in dozens of ways, great and small, he supported the institution. By buying and selling sugar produced by slave labor in the Caribbean, for instance, Woolman was indirectly sustaining slavery, and by writing wills for local slaveholders that disposed of slaves as if they were horses, Woolman believed he was doing the same.

By the 1750s, Woolman's conscience had begun to bother him considerably. In response, he began reducing his involvement with slavery. He refused to write wills that disposed of slave property; he stopped buying, selling, and using sugar. Since dyes were generally manufactured by slave workers, Woolman even stopped dyeing his clothes. During a journey through the South in 1757 Woolman left money behind for the slaves who served him. But Woolman's concerns for slaves went well beyond a desire to remain pure and uninvolved with the institution. By writing, publishing, and speaking out against slavery, Woolman challenged Americans to think deeply about the institution and to examine their own consciences with patience, compassion, and care.

Eighteenth-century Quaker John Woolman was a staunch opponent of slavery.

human beings—men, women, and children with rights and feelings; thus, it was wrong to participate in slavery. "Those who steal or robb men, and those who buy or purchase them," these Quakers argued, "are they not all alike?"[22]

The Germantown statement set the tone for later protests. Over the next several decades, dozens of Quakers and Quaker groups published their own attacks on slavery. Like the Quakers of Germantown, most of these reformers argued primarily that slavery was immoral and unjust. In a 1693 pamphlet, for example, Quaker writer George Keith highlighted the cruelties of slavery and argued that a fair society would never permit such abuse. "Many that buy [slaves] do exceedingly afflict and oppress them," he wrote, "not only by continual hard Labour, but by cruel Whippings, and other cruel Punishments."[23]

Other antislavery advocates echoed these concerns. "The Colour of a Man avails nothing, in Matters of Right and Equity," observed Quaker writer John Woolman in a book published in 1754. "To consider mankind otherwise than Brethren, to think Favours are peculiar to one Nation . . . plainly supposes a Darkness [ignorance] in the Understanding."[24] This argument directly stated the Quaker principle that all people were equals. Color, race, and nationality did not matter. What counted, instead, was humanity, and in the world of the Quakers, slaves were as human as everyone else.

However, the early Quaker abolitionists did not rely exclusively on appeals to compassion and morality. They also relied on the Bible to buttress their antislavery arguments. While acknowledging the proslavery slant of several Biblical passages, George Keith and other Friends highlighted verses that seemed to tell a different story. In his pamphlet, for instance, Keith quoted Exodus 22:21, "Thou shalt neither vex a stranger nor oppress him," and went on to add: "But what greater Oppressions can there be inflicted upon our Felow Creatures, than is inflicted upon the poor Negroes!" God, Keith insisted, would surely take revenge against those who showed no mercy toward the "afflicted tormented miserable Slaves!"[25]

Other Reformers

The Quakers may have represented the first organized opposition to slavery in North America, but they were not alone. In 1701,

Massachusetts judge Samuel Sewall (left) and writer George Keith (right) vehemently argued that the Bible did not advocate slavery.

for example, a Massachusetts judge named Samuel Sewall wrote and published an antislavery pamphlet of his own. Like Keith and other Quaker commentators, Sewall argued that the Bible did not condone slavery. In particular, Sewall asserted that the New Testament superseded the proslavery verses in the Hebrew Bible. The words of Jesus, Sewall explained, called Christians to treat others as they wished to be treated themselves. That meant recognizing the essential humanity of all persons, even slaves—who, Sewall reflected, were "the Offspring of God [and] ought to be treated with a Respect agreeable."[26]

Sewall also relied on moral principles to make his case against slavery. Although he did not deny that European civilizations and religions were superior to those of Africa, he sharply criticized the notion, expressed by the defenders of slavery, that the institution was acceptable because it exposed Africans to Western ways. "Evil must not be done, that good may come of it,"[27] he observed. In the same way, Sewall was quick to denounce the slave trade on ethical grounds. "It is likewise most lamentable to think," he wrote, "how in taking Negroes out of Africa, and selling of them here, That which God has joined together, Men do boldly rend asunder; Men from their Country, Husbands from their Wives, Parents from their Children."[28]

During the next few decades, Sewall's arguments were taken up and repeated by other non-Quaker reformers. Some emphasized Sewall's Biblical evidence in their opposition to slavery; others preferred to stress the cruelty, immorality, or injustice of the institution. A few argued against slavery on the basis of self-interest, warning of slave rebellions or the high financial costs of holding slaves. The risk of revolt seemed particularly strong to some. Slavery, fretted one group of colonists in 1739, "would oblige us to keep a Guard-duty at least as severe as [if] we expected a daily Invasion."[29]

But whether they belonged to the Society of Friends, like Keith and Woolman, or to the mainstream Puritan or Anglican faiths, like Samuel Sewall, the impact of the first abolitionists was relatively small. Until about 1760, most Americans simply did not care one way or the other about slavery. Consequently, the writings of Keith, Woolman, Sewall, and other reformers had little immediate effect.

The Enlightenment

In the 1760s, though, the widespread apathy toward slavery would finally begin to change, in large part because of a philosophical movement as the result of a period known as the Enlightenment. A product of eighteenth-century Western Europe, the Enlightenment represented a revolution in thought. During this time, philosophers came to value science and reason, order and logic. In particular, many European thinkers came to believe in certain "natural laws" that governed and underlay every aspect of the universe. These laws applied not merely to astronomy, physics, and other sciences, but to human behavior and morality as well. According to the thinkers of the Enlightenment, these natural laws established in particular that human beings should be free, equal, and self-governing.

This notion had important implications where slavery was concerned. Many people of the Enlightenment found it impossible to accept the doctrine of natural laws while at the same time accepting the existence of slavery. Years earlier, men like Keith,

Sewall, and Woolman had argued that slavery violated basic principles of morality. Now, a new generation found itself in agreement. "The God of nature gave [us] life and freedom," argued a group of slaves in New Hampshire in 1779, "upon the terms of the most perfect equality with other men."[30]

The ideas of the Enlightenment, moreover, formed the basis of the American Revolution, the war in which the United States ceased to be British territory and became instead an independent

Thomas Jefferson, Benjamin Franklin, and others draft the Declaration of Independence. The existence of slavery in the colonies contradicted the Declaration's assertion that all men are created equal.

nation. As the colonists saw it, the Revolution was a battle to win the natural right of self-government. "We hold these truths to be self-evident," wrote Thomas Jefferson in the Declaration of Independence, using language that would have been familiar to any

Phillis Wheatley

◼

Phillis Wheatley was born about 1753 in West Africa and brought to Massachusetts by a slave trader in 1761. Purchased by a kind and caring couple who gave her an education and treated her much like their own child, Wheatley won her freedom as a young woman. She earned widespread fame as a poet. Some of her verses were well in keeping with the themes of the early abolition movement, as is demonstrated by this excerpt, quoted in Mason Lowance, ed., *Against Slavery: An Abolitionist Reader:*

Should you, my lord, while you peruse my song,
Wonder from whence my love of Freedom sprung,
Whence flow these wishes for the common good,
By feeling hearts best understood,
I, young in life, by seeming cruel fate
Was snatched from Afric's fancied happy seat:
What pangs excruciating must molest,
What sorrows labor in my parent's breast?
Steeled was that soul and by no misery moved
That from a father seized his babe beloved:
Such, such my case. And can I then but pray
Others may never feel tyrannic sway?

Phyllis Wheatley earned lasting fame as a free black poet. Much of her work condemns the institution of slavery.

Enlightenment philosopher, "that all men are created equal; that they are endowed by their Creator with certain unalienable Rights, that among these are Life, Liberty, and the pursuit of Happiness."[31]

There was, of course, an enormous contradiction between these words and the existence of slavery, and many of the Revolution's supporters recognized it. If all men were created equal, it was unacceptable to hold some in bondage. In particular, if the colonists were struggling for their own liberty, some Americans realized, they could not conscientiously deny their slaves the same goal. In 1774, for example, Abigail Adams, the wife of John Adams, later to be the second president of the United States, wrote, "It has always seemed a most iniquitous scheme to me to fight ourselves for what we are daily robbing and plundering from those who have as good a right to freedom as we have."[32]

Steps Toward Abolition

During the Revolution, at least for a time, abolitionist sentiment seemed widespread. Even in the South, where the institution was the strongest, many influential planters were expressing their distaste for slavery. "There is not a man living who wishes more sincerely than I do to see a plan adopted for the abolition of [slavery]," wrote George Washington. "An evil exists which desires a remedy."[33] And in the North, where slavery had never been common, antislavery opinion helped eliminate the institution altogether. Beginning in 1777, one Northern jurisdiction after another passed laws restricting and then abolishing the ownership of slaves. By 1804, the process of emancipation had begun in every Northern state and had been completed in many.

Still, the changing moral attitudes about slavery were not enough to destroy the institution altogether. Even in the North, the emancipation of the slaves had less to do with the ideas of Revolution and the Enlightenment than it did with economic considerations. Though agricultural slaves had little to do during the long Northern winters, their owners had to feed, clothe, and house them year-round. In the end, it simply proved cheaper for Northern farmers to pay wages to day laborers. Self-interest, not ethical concerns or Enlightenment principles, was what led most Northerners to give up their slaves.

And in the South, good intentions were not enough. Despite the attitudes of powerful Southerners such as Washington, slavery did not vanish through the South following the Revolution. On the contrary, it grew. By 1800, new methods of farming across the South had led to a greater demand for slaves. Even Southerners who questioned the morality of slavery found it difficult to ignore the financial advantages that owning slaves could bring them. As the nineteenth century began, slavery had become a major force throughout the Southern states.

The work of the colonial and Revolutionary abolitionists, though, had not been in vain. Though they had not defeated the institution of slavery, they had spoken out against it. They had raised thoughtful objections to the slave system; they had attacked it on grounds that were at once moral, spiritual, and practical. Some fifty years after the Revolutionary era, when abolitionism once again burst onto the scene, the revitalized movement would owe much to the writings and ideals of the antislavery activists who fought the institution in the 1600s and 1700s.

Chapter Three

The Rise of a New Movement

The antislavery movement continued to lobby for abolition throughout the Federal period—roughly, the years between the ratification of the Constitution in 1788 and the presidency of Andrew Jackson, who took office in 1828. The reformers of this time did experience a few victories, among them an 1808 ban on the importation of slaves and an 1820 measure that prohibited slavery in U.S. territories north and west of Missouri. But for the most part, the abolition movement languished during these years. Poorly organized, easily ignored, and beaten back by the changes in Southern farming that made slavery more profitable than it had previously been, the reformers seemed unable to get their message across.

Then, without warning, the antislavery movement completely altered its direction, its methods, and even its goals. The changes were dramatic, sudden, and unexpected. In 1828, the movement had been dominated by mild, peaceable reformers who gently nagged slaveholders to change their ways and politely offered to educate Northerners about the realities of slavery. Within just three or four years, these leaders had been pushed aside by brash, headstrong champions of the slave: men and women who made demands rather than requests, who scorned

A crew aboard a slave ship hangs a black woman upside down by her ankle. The first aim of abolitionists was to expose the violent realities of slavery.

and reviled their opponents, who banded together to establish organization after organization dedicated to their cause. All at once, the abolitionist movement was transformed.

Walker's Appeal

The changes in the abolitionist movement were unplanned and largely spontaneous. No single activist was solely, or even primarily, responsible for setting the movement on a new course; no single event marked the new era's beginning. One possible starting point, however, was the publication in 1829 of a small book on slavery written by a free black man named David Walker. Originally titled *Appeal to the Coloured Citizens of the World*—today, it is better known as *Walker's Appeal*—the book was a bitter attack on slavery and all that it stood for. Walker's work represented a sharp departure from the circumspect writings on slavery that had marked the previous era. It would set the tone for future reformers.

Walker had never been a slave. He had been born into freedom in North Carolina in 1785. Nonetheless, through personal observation he had come to know the slave system quite well. As a young man, he had traveled extensively through the South, where he had seen firsthand the brutality inflicted upon the slaves. What he observed saddened him, but mostly, it made him furious. Around 1815, discouraged and angered by the realities of the South, Walker left North Carolina for good and moved to Boston. "It [is] a great trial for me to live on the same soil where so many men are in slavery," he wrote; "certainly I cannot remain where I must hear their chains constantly."[34]

Though *Walker's Appeal* was short, it attacked slavery from many different perspectives. For example, Walker refuted the notion that slavery was justified by the Bible, along with the contention that blacks were of inferior intelligence to whites. In a similar vein, Walker noted the contradictions between the lofty ideals of the Declaration of Independence and the abuses of the slave system. "I ask you candidly," he wrote, addressing white Americans, "[were] your sufferings under Great Britain one hundredth part as cruel and tyrannical as you have rendered ours under you?"[35]

But Walker's real purpose was not in demolishing the intellectual arguments of the slaveholders, nor even in appealing to the kindness of those who perpetuated slavery. Instead, *Walker's Appeal* was an impassioned indictment of an institution that systematically oppressed and degraded black people. "The whites have always been an unjust, jealous, unmerciful, avaricious and blood-thirsty set of beings,"[36] he wrote. While most previous writers had avoided discussing slavery in emotional terms, Walker's work seethed with anger, frustration, and despair.

Walker's book included one other important feature—an advocacy of violent resistance to slavery. At several points in his narrative, Walker insisted that slaves should fight back against their masters. "It is no more harm for you to kill a man, who is trying to kill you," he wrote, "than it is to take a drink of water when thirsty."[37] Walker knew that a slave who struck back with violence would swiftly be put to death. For this reason, Walker urged slaves to strike suddenly and without hesitation. "If you commence . . . ," he advised, "Do not trifle, for they will not trifle with you."[38]

Reaction

Walker's Appeal was extremely controversial. Southerners, in particular, objected to Walker's tone and questioned his facts. And almost all readers, Northerners and Southerners alike, were put off by Walker's open advocacy of violence. Still, *Walker's Appeal* found a following. Unlike many of his predecessors, Walker wrote from the heart. His work was impassioned, raw, and powerful in a way that earlier antislavery documents were not. In addition, Walker's personal experience with slavery provided a contrast to the work of many earlier abolitionists. "I do not speak from hearsay," Walker explained; "what I have written, is what I have seen and heard myself."[39]

Whether people agreed with Walker or not, the impact of the book was undeniable. Walker had succeeded in stirring up controversy across the country. It seemed that abolition was on everyone's lips. Before the publication of the *Appeal*, the antislavery movement had been calm and moderate, polite and accommodating—and generally unsuccessful in getting people to pay attention. Now, at last, people were becoming aware of the movement. True, much of the reaction was hostile, but some activists, weary of not being taken seriously, were thrilled that one of their number was being noticed at all.

An Attack on Gradualism

In his work, Walker took particular pains to take a stand on two important issues. The first, known as gradualism, or gradual abolition, was a doctrine accepted by most abolitionists before the publication of Walker's book. As the name implied, this doctrine held that slavery should be eliminated over time rather than all at once. During and after the American Revolution, gradualism had been the method used to free the slaves in several Northern states, including Pennsylvania and New York, and many antislavery activists of the early 1800s thought it would prove equally effective in the South.

Gradualists had several reasons for rejecting the idea of immediate abolition. For one, they argued that chaos would result if the slaves were freed all at once. Few slaves were ready for liberty, they claimed, and slaveholders would protest any immediate confiscation of their slaves. With time and effort, though, the gradualists asserted, these details could be worked out. Slaves

A Vivid Writer

■

David Walker was an extremely vivid writer, given to frequent use of capital letters, italics, and strings of up to eight exclamation points. The passage excerpted below, quoted in Charles M. Wiltse's edition of *Walker's Appeal*, is a particularly striking example of Walker's writing style and method of argument.

In that Island [Jamaica], there are three hundred and fifty thousand souls—of whom fifteen thousand are whites, the remainder, three hundred and thirty-five thousand[,] are coloured people! and this Island is ruled by the white people!!!!!!!! (15,000) ruling and tyranizing over 335,000 persons!!!!!!!!—O! coloured men!! O! coloured men!!! O! coloured men!!!! Look!! Look!!! at this!!!! and, tell me if we are not abject and servile enough, how long, O! how long my colour [black Americans] shall we be dupes and dogs to the cruel whites?

could be educated; masters could be convinced that abolition was right and proper. In truth, the emancipation schemes of many gradualists were lacking in detail. Some set arbitrary dates in the future upon which all slaves would be free; others spoke vaguely of financial incentives to masters willing to emancipate their slaves. All, however, were firmly convinced that abolition was inevitable. Within a generation or two, the gradualists believed, slavery in the South would have withered away.

But though gradualism was accepted by most abolitionists of the Federal period, Walker emphatically rejected it. Instead, he argued for immediate emancipation of all slaves. He was not the first American abolitionist to do so; in 1817, for instance, an activist named John Kenrick had mocked gradual abolition by likening it to "gradually leaving off piracy[,] murder [or] adultery."[40] Still, *Walker's Appeal* struck a particular nerve among many who read it. If slavery was indeed as dehumanizing, brutal, and unjust as Walker described it, these readers reasoned, then it was immoral to ask the slaves to wait for their freedom.

"Plot of Satan"

The other issue Walker discussed was a plan known as colonization, which was accepted at the time by most abolitionists as a way of dealing with the former slaves. One stumbling block faced by the early antislavery activists was the racism prevalent across America, both in the North and in the South. Few white Americans had any desire to live near blacks, especially if that meant accepting them in any way as social equals. And virtually no whites wished to compete for jobs with African Americans. If emancipation meant swarms of uneducated, unskilled blacks roaming the country—and to many Americans of the Federal period, that was exactly what the term implied—then the abolition movement seemed doomed to failure.

The concept of colonization was an answer to this objection. Under this plan, newly freed slaves would be sent to Africa to found a new country based on Western principles. In their ancestral homeland, blacks could live in freedom and peace. Colonization schemes allowed Northern whites to support emancipation without fearing a deluge of former slaves. Moreover, abolitionists noted, many moderate slaveholders embraced the principles of colonization. Colonization, in short, seemed capable of solving the entire problem of American slavery.

But Walker vigorously attacked the principle of colonization, which he termed a "cunningly devised plot of Satan."[41] Walker believed that colonization plans were based on racism, and he did not hesitate to say so. He felt that American whites had the obligation to educate the slaves after having oppressed them so long, and he argued that colonization was simply a clever way for slaveholders to avoid this duty. Finally, Walker pointed out that many black leaders had expressed deep dismay over colonization plans, and for good reason. Africa, by this time, had become alien territory for blacks whose ancestors had arrived in America two centuries ago. "This country is as much ours as it is the whites[']," Walker wrote, "whether they will admit it now or not."[42]

Walker's biting attacks on both gradualism and colonization distressed some antislavery activists but thrilled others. Just as they had been drawn to Walker's emotional appeals and his personal knowledge of slavery, some reformers admired Walker's uncompromising stance for immediate abolition without colonization. Walker's anger and radical ideas may have been jarring to some activists, but they encouraged and emboldened others. Over the next few years, a succession of militant, emotional, and adamant reformers would step forward to carry on the quest for freedom. The time for quiet, reasoned debate had passed. A moral crusade against slavery had begun.

A New Generation

The abolitionists of the 1830s and beyond were quite different from their predecessors in many ways. The antislavery movement that preceded Walker had been dominated by Quakers, but though Quakers continued to play a role in the movement after 1830, they no longer set the tone. Now, the reformers included a broad assortment of people from various backgrounds. Some

A crowd of abolitionists listens as a speaker rails against the evils of slavery. A family of free blacks can be seen in the lower right of this illustration.

Sarah Grimké, Angelina Grimké Weld, and Ohio lecturer Theodore Weld (from left) played central roles in the emerging abolitionist movement of the 1830s.

were young men and women, new to the movement and to activism in general; others were veteran reformers eager to find a more effective way of spreading their message. These activists all approached slavery from different perspectives, but they were united in their opposition to the institution.

Like David Walker, many of these new activists were African American. The involvement of American blacks in abolition efforts was nothing new. During both colonial times and the Federal period, free blacks had often been strong voices against slavery. "Can I then but pray," wrote Phillis Wheatley, a freed slave and poet of the Revolutionary era, "others may never feel tyrannic sway?"[43] But in the 1830s, the importance and visibility of black abolitionists increased dramatically. African American reformers such as Frederick Douglass, traveling preacher Sojourner Truth, and escaped slave Harriet Tubman, among many others, became well known across the country.

Not all the abolitionists were African American, of course. Indeed, despite the contributions of Douglass, Tubman, and others, the new movement, like the old, was led mainly by white men. Some of these, such as brothers Arthur and Lewis Tappan of New York City, were well-off business leaders. Others, like Theodore Dwight Weld, were Protestant ministers. William Lloyd

Garrison was a newspaper editor, John Greenleaf Whittier a poet, and Horace Mann an educator. Nearly all of these white male abolitionists came from the Northern states. A few had Southern roots as well; Levi Coffin, for instance, who played a major role in helping slaves to escape, spent much of his early life in North Carolina, and publisher and politician James Birney, born in Kentucky, had owned slaves in Alabama as a young man.

White women, too, played a vital role in the new abolitionist movement. Sarah and Angelina Grimké, sisters who had grown up on a South Carolina plantation, were among the white women who participated in the movement; Angelina would later marry the antislavery preacher Theodore Weld. Novelist Harriet Beecher Stowe, who wrote the best-selling novel *Uncle Tom's Cabin*, was another well-known female abolitionist. So was novelist and essayist Lydia Maria Child. Like the African American abolitionists, the white women who worked for the antislavery cause did not usually hold positions of leadership in abolitionist societies. Still, by speaking out frequently against the evils of slavery, they too spread the message of abolition.

Wherever this new generation of abolitionists came from, whatever their race or gender, they were eager to organize. Once, the various strands of the movement had remained disconnected.

England's Experience

Throughout their struggle against slavery, American abolitionists were strongly influenced by their counterparts in Great Britain. Although slavery never gained much of a foothold in England itself, British business interests benefited from the slave trade and from goods made by slaves in British colonies. But as the Enlightenment took shape, British thinkers began to seriously question slavery and British involvement in it. "Do you never *feel* another's pain?" demanded English cleric John Wesley of the slave traders in 1774, quoted in David Brion Davis, *The Problem of Slavery in Western Culture.* "When you saw the flowing eyes . . . or the bleeding sides or tortured limbs of your fellow-creatures . . . did not one tear drop from your eye?"

Just like the American abolitionists, the British abolitionists relied on descriptions of the cruelties of slavery and on language that reflected moral and religious objections to holding others in bondage. The British experience, however, was very different from the experiences of the American abolitionists. Unlike in America, there was no single large group of influential leaders dedicated to preserving the institution of slavery. As a result, in 1833, Britain passed a bill outlawing slavery in all its possessions, notably in its colonies throughout the Caribbean. By 1838, when the law actually took effect, slavery in the British Empire was finished. The banning of slavery throughout the British Empire gave a tremendous boost to the American abolitionists.

Now, reformers hurried to join forces and to coordinate their efforts. Abolition societies soon sprang up across the North, some of them large indeed. The most influential, the American Anti-Slavery Society, which was founded in 1833 by advocates of immediate emancipation, would eventually number a quarter million members in over a thousand chapters. The emphasis on collaboration gave reformers a strength they had never had before.

"I WILL BE HEARD"

What most marked the new abolition movement, however, was neither its organization nor its diversity, but its rhetoric. The new generation of reformers enthusiastically echoed David Walker's emotion, militancy, and rage. "On this subject [that is, slavery]," thundered William Lloyd Garrison in the first issue of his abolitionist newspaper *The Liberator*, "I do not wish to think, or speak, or write, with moderation." A recent convert—thanks in part to Walker—to the cause of immediate abolition, Garrison meant exactly what he said. "I will not equivocate," he added. "I will not excuse— I will not retreat a single inch—AND I WILL BE HEARD."[44]

Garrison was not the only strident voice for change. In an 1839 book, Theodore Weld used Walker-style language to describe the cruelties of slavery and to indict those who remained apathetic to its injustice. "Slavery is a curse," he wrote. "Whoever denies this, his lips libel his heart. Try him; clank the chains in his ears, and tell then that they are for *him*. Give him an hour to prepare his wife and children for a lifetime of slavery. Bid him make haste and get ready their necks for the yoke . . . then look at his pale lips and trembling knees, and you have *nature's* testimony against slavery."[45] In the abolitionist movement, white men like Weld and Garrison had no monopoly on sharp rhetoric and angry words. "Let your motto be resistance! *resistance!* RESISTANCE!"[46] cried African American preacher Henry Highland Garnet, urging the slaves to rebel. Antislavery women, too, were equally capable of speaking and writing with passion and forcefulness. "What an appalling spectacle do we now present!" wrote Weld's sister-in-law, Sarah Grimké. "With one hand we clasp the cross of Christ, and with the other grasp the neck of the downtrodden slave!"[47]

Such images and language were shocking to many Americans. But for many abolitionists, creating a shock was precisely the point. Their purpose was to shame the slaveholders and to shake Northerners out of their apathy toward the institution. The best way to achieve those goals, they reasoned, was to go on the offensive. The days of gentle persuasion were done; it was time to reveal slavery for the dreadful tradition it was. "I WILL BE HEARD,"[48] William Lloyd Garrison had cried, and he and his fellow abolitionists would make sure that people listened.

Chapter Four

One Cause, Many Voices

The abolitionist reformers of the 1830s and beyond were a diverse group of people. White and black, male and female, Midwesterner and New Englander, Quaker and Anglican—these activists came from distinct backgrounds, held varying ideals, and wrote and spoke with differing styles. In many ways, this diversity strengthened the cause of abolition. Because of the breadth of the movement, the reformers presented a powerful force when they could put aside their differences and act together in pursuit of their common goal.

But at other times, the movement's diversity presented a challenge. Given the varying opinions and personalities that made up the abolition movement, disagreement was inevitable. Former slaves and well-heeled whites argued about the movement's priorities; preachers and editors disputed methods and strategies. This dissension distracted the abolitionists from their goal and weakened the movement. The multiplicity of voices in the movement during this time, then, was at once the reformers' greatest strength and their greatest curse.

Arguments Against Slavery

In keeping with the diversity of the movement, the abolitionist leaders of the pre–Civil War years formulated a variety of arguments against slavery. One of the most important of these arguments involved ancient cultures. The fact that earlier civilizations had accepted slavery had always been an important justification of the institution, but as the 1800s wore on, some Americans deepened and refined this argument. More and more, proslavery thinkers suggested that slavery had actually helped create the great civilizations of earlier times. To slavery alone, theorized slaveholder George Fitzhugh, "Greece and Rome, Egypt and Judea, and all the other distinguished States of antiquity, were indebted for their great prosperity and high civilization."[49]

Now, however, abolitionists attacked that notion. Activist Lydia Maria Child, for instance, argued that Southern slaves were not at all comparable to those of earlier cultures. Greek slaves, she noted, had the right to escape an abusive master; the Hebrews sometimes made slaves their heirs. Although the slaves held by these and other civilizations may not have been treated kindly, they nevertheless enjoyed rights and protections not offered to the slaves of the South. "The fact is," Child concluded, "negro-slavery is totally different from any other form of bondage that ever existed."[50]

Activist Lydia Maria Child argued that Southern slaves endured harsher treatment than the slaves of the ancient world.

Abolitionists of the time also appealed to more recent historical events, notably the Revolution and the signing of the Declaration of Independence. For many reformers, the Declaration, in particular, remained an especially fresh and vibrant document, and they cited its principles frequently. They admired the Declaration's noble language, its uncompromising ideals, and its clear statement of the fundamental equality of all people. Antislavery activists routinely reminded their audiences of the connection between their work and the Declaration, and most took great pleasure in pointing out the contradictions in the thinking of those who professed to love the Declaration but nonetheless supported slavery.

Slavery As It Was

Other abolitionists of the pre–Civil War era spent their time describing the evils of slavery. David Walker had done this to excellent effect in his *Appeal*; now, others took up where he had left off. The former slaves active in the movement were invaluable in this role. To them, slavery was real and immediate in a way it could never be for white abolitionists. Escaped slaves thus provided audiences with a unique perspective on the slave system as practiced in the South. Far better than anyone else, they could describe what it *felt* like to be a slave.

For many Northerners, the words of these former slaves were compelling. It was one thing to read a book that presented intellectual arguments against the slave system; it was quite another for an audience to see firsthand the scars that lined the backs of many former slaves. Although many of these abolitionists were most effective when speaking directly to an audience, their writings, too, had the power to stir emotion. As Frederick Douglass wrote of a former master, "[He] lashed me till he had worn out his switches, cutting me so savagely as to leave the marks visible for a long time."[51]

Black abolitionists, however, were not the only reformers to catalog the brutality of the slave system. In a book published in 1836, for example, Lydia Maria Child reprinted several chilling reports of slavery told to her by Southern planters and by Northerners who had traveled in the South. Issues of William Lloyd Garrison's *The Liberator* newspaper often included similar descriptions. And Harriet Beecher Stowe's novel *Uncle Tom's Cabin* included fictional scenes of violence that were based on the actual experiences of runaway slaves.

The most thorough recitation of slavery's horrors, though, appeared in 1839 in a book by Ohio preacher and lecturer

Publisher William Lloyd Garrison cataloged the brutality of slavery in his abolitionist newspaper, *The Liberator.*

Theodore Weld. Titled *American Slavery As It Is: Testimony of a Thousand Witnesses*, the book was essentially a compendium of brutalities suffered by slaves. A careful researcher, Weld gathered his information from a multitude of sources, including the accounts of Northern travelers and the recollections of former slaves. With the assistance of his wife, Angelina Grimké Weld, and her sister, Sarah Grimké, Weld also scoured Southern newspapers for evidence that could be used to indict the slave system.

The result was a systematic record of slavery's horrors. One section of the book, for instance, consisted entirely of over a hundred runaway slave advertisements culled from Southern papers. Each ad sought the return of an escaped slave, who—according to the description given—had been maimed, stabbed, shot, or otherwise assaulted by his or her master. "A few days before she went off, I burnt her with a hot iron, on the left side of her face," read the first advertisement in the group; "I tried to make the letter 'M.'"[52] Weld's intent was to overwhelm the reader with the realities of the slave system, and in that goal he was wildly successful.

When describing slaveholder brutality, the abolitionists usually focused on the beatings and other punishments given the slaves. Those were the most appalling examples of mistreatment and therefore provoked the most horror and outrage among audiences. But the reformers also took pains to describe other aspects of the slaves' lives. Douglass, for instance, spoke frequently about the amount of work planters expected of the slaves. And Weld, Garrison, and others discussed the inadequate food, clothing, and shelter the slaves received, along with the meager protection offered the slaves by state and local laws. "In North Carolina," pointed out Lydia Maria Child, "the law decides that a quart of corn per day is sufficient. But, if the slave does not receive this poor allowance, who can *prove* the fact[?]"[53]

The Religious Argument

Perhaps the most common argument used by the abolitionists during this time, however, involved neither history nor recitations of slavery's brutality. Instead, it had to do with religion. Most of the antislavery activists of the 1830s and beyond were deeply religious. Theodore Weld was just one of many preachers involved in the movement. Most other activists of the time, from novelist Harriet Beecher Stowe to editor William Lloyd Garrison, were evangelical Protestants by birth and by inclination. These men and women knew their Bible—and were strongly influenced by Christian theology. Their faith, then, was evident in their antislavery work.

As earlier advocates had discovered, the Bible had many verses that indicated approval of slavery, but comparatively few that were obviously hostile to the institution. Although it was therefore difficult to base their case on the Bible alone, some abolitionists tried. Theodore Weld, for example, argued that the Eighth Commandment (Exodus 2:15, "Thou shalt not steal") was fundamentally abolitionist in its outlook. "The eighth commandment presupposes and assumes the right of every man to his powers, and their product," Weld observed. "Slavery robs [him] of both."[54]

In general, the abolitionists were on more solid footing when they discussed the New Testament than when they cited evidence from the Hebrew Bible. Here, following the ideas expressed over a century earlier by Samuel Sewall, the reformers' argument rested less on specific passages and more on the overarching theme of love and forgiveness found in the Gospels. "It is the *spirit* of the Holy Word, not its particular *expressions*," wrote Lydia Maria Child, "which must be a rule for our conduct. How can slavery be reconciled with the maxim, 'Do unto others, as ye would that others should do unto you?'"[55]

"Filled with the Spirit of Christ"

The ideas expressed by Child formed the heart of the reformers' appeal to religion. The abolitionists of the time simply could not reconcile their view of Christianity with the existence of slavery. Not only were they certain that slavery was a sin, they were equally certain that Jesus would have seen the institution in precisely the same way. Slavery, then, was in direct opposition to basic Christian ideals. As the antislavery activists saw it, God was on the abolitionists' side.

This idea underscored most of the rhetoric of the antislavery movement. Abolitionists frequently justified their work by declaring that God demanded the emancipation of the slaves. "God . . . is waiting to see whether we will hearken unto his voice," wrote Sarah Grimké in an open letter to Southern clergymen. "He has sent out his light and his truth."[56] William Lloyd Garrison put it even more bluntly. "We would be filled with the spirit of CHRIST," he wrote; "we purpose, in a moral and spiritual sense, to speak and act boldly in the cause of GOD."[57]

Christianity and Slavery

One of the bitterest debates between the abolitionists and the radical Southern defenders of slavery involved the religious basis of slavery, an important question because practically all Americans of the mid-nineteenth century were devoted Christians. Southerners insisted that the Bible supported the institution; abolitionists, in turn, believed that the principles of Christianity were diametrically opposed to slavery. "It is the tendency and design of the Christian religion, when fairly applied," asserted reformist Albert Barnes in his 1846 book *An Inquiry into the Scriptural Views of Slavery*, "to abolish the system [of slavery]."

The intensity of this debate helped the abolitionists create some of their most sharply worded and most heartfelt arguments against slavery. "Have we nothing to do with slavery?" asked white preacher James Freeman Clarke in an attempt to rouse Northern Christians from their apathy toward the institution, quoted in Mason Lowance, ed., *Against Slavery: An Abolitionist Reader.* "Is not our neighbor the suffering man . . . ? Ought we not to love him as ourselves? Shall Mason and Dixon's line [the boundary between South and North] be an insurmountable barrier to our Christian sympathies?"

The abolitionists also attacked the Bible-based arguments of the Southerners. "Among other apologies for slavery," Lydia Maria Child tartly observed in her *Appeal in Favor of That Class of Americans Called Africans*, "it has been asserted that the Bible does not forbid it. Neither does it forbid the counterfeiting of a bank-bill." Some activists charged that the defenders of slavery mistranslated the original words of the Bible to make their case. When all else failed, the reformers turned to mockery. "Some of the Bible defences thrown around slavery," commented Theodore Weld, quoted in Lowance, *Against Slavery,* " . . . do so torture common sense, Scripture, and historical fact, that it [is] hard to tell whether absurdity, fatuity [foolishness], ignorance or blasphemy, predominates."

The abolitionists of the time also combined their religious ideas with the ethical principles of the Enlightenment. To the reformers, God's law and natural law were one and the same. "Man has rights by nature," stated preacher William Ellery Channing. "These are gifts of the Creator, not grants of society."[58] This notion showed up most clearly in the abolitionists' insistence that all people, including slaves, were the same in the eyes of God. "B is a Brother with a skin / Of somewhat darker hue," wrote one activist in an abolitionist alphabet book, designed to instruct white children in the tenets of the movement. "But in our Heavenly Father's sight / He is as dear as you."[59]

The reformers' religious arguments sometimes took on a warning tone. Protestant theology of the time taught that God, while kind and just, had a great capacity for anger and revenge. The reformers urged slaveholders to see the errors of their ways and warned of dreadful consequences if they did not. "Can any thing be a greater mockery of religion than the way in which it is conducted by [white] Americans?" cried David Walker. "I call God— I call angels—I call men, to witness, that your [white Americans'] DESTRUCTION *is at hand*, and will be speedily consummated unless you REPENT."[60]

The Underground Railroad

The abolitionists directed much of their energy toward argument and debate. Experienced writers and speakers, they were most at home in the world of words; from 1830 to the end of slavery in 1865, they flooded the country with documents, speeches, and other materials designed to express their opinions and convert Americans to their cause. But not all members of the movement were devoted exclusively to convincing a nation or to expressing a point of view. Instead of agitating for the emancipation of slaves, some men and women chose to spend their time helping the slaves free themselves.

With no legal means of earning their freedom, slaves could escape their bondage only by running away, and many dreamed of doing exactly that. "I will run away," Frederick Douglass remembered thinking at one point during his youth. "I will not stand it. Get caught or get clear, I'll try it."[61] Unfortunately for the slaves, making a successful escape was extraordinarily difficult.

Freedom lay in the North, but the North was simply too far away for all except those who lived in one of the border states—the northernmost tier of slave states, from Delaware to Missouri. Even those who lived close enough to make escape a possibility had to travel by night through forests and swamps, avoiding armed patrols and constantly searching for food and shelter. Many slaves tried to escape to freedom; few succeeded.

The abolitionists, however, did what they could to help. By 1830, many antislavery activists had banded together into a loose network known as the Underground Railroad. In keeping with the railroad metaphor, these abolitionists—a mix of free blacks and white reformers—were known as "conductors." They provided fugitive slaves with money, food, and shelter. Many of them hid runaways in their own homes; then, when the time was right, they directed the runaways to another safe house further north. In that way, slaves could travel from one sympathizer to another until they reached the North.

Since the Underground Railroad was shadowy and unofficial, it had no single leader. There were, however, several important

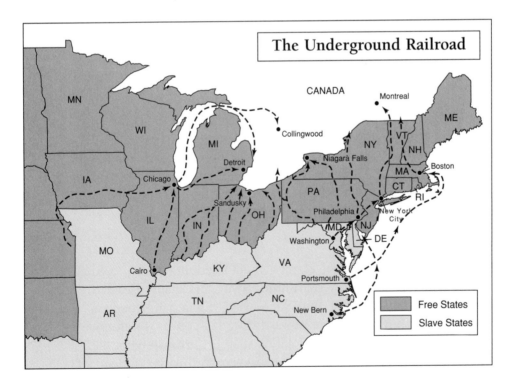

The Underground Railroad

Harriet Tubman (far left) helped this slave family escape to freedom. More than three hundred slaves escaped thanks to Tubman's efforts.

organizers whose efforts were invaluable to the network. William Still, for instance, was a black man living in Philadelphia, the first destination of many slaves from the East Coast. Still helped newly arrived fugitives move further north and find jobs. A white Quaker named Levi Coffin was another famous conductor and leader, whose untiring efforts on behalf of the slaves earned him the informal title of "the president of the Underground Railroad."[62] According to some estimates, as many as three thousand fugitives passed through safe houses he established in Indiana and Ohio.

The most famous person associated with the Underground Railroad, however, was Harriet Tubman. A native of Maryland, Tubman escaped from slavery in 1849, assisted in part by the organization. Soon after reaching Philadelphia, she resolved to return to the slave territory to guide other fugitives to safety. This was an extremely dangerous move, since recapture would have meant a swift return to slavery. Still, Tubman did not hesitate. As historians Charles Johnson and Patricia Smith report, "She returned to the South at least nineteen times to rescue her own family and more than three hundred other captives."[63]

Discord

Tubman, Coffin, and the other conductors on the Underground Railroad were attacking slavery in the way they believed they could do the most good. So, for that matter, were the other members of the movement: newspaper editors such as William Lloyd Garrison, speakers like Frederick Douglass, politicians such as James Birney. In theory, at least, the various efforts of the abolitionist movement complemented and supported each other. At their best, preachers and politicians coexisted peacefully and encouraged each other's work. Ideally, the men and women, whites and blacks, who made up the abolition movement were able to put aside their differences and join together for a greater goal.

But the abolitionists were an extraordinarily diverse group of people. The reformers ran the gamut from former slaves, born into extreme poverty and oppression, to well-off former slaveholders; from evangelical Protestant preachers from the rural Midwest to Quakers from urban Pennsylvania; from men, accustomed to holding power in reform movements, to women, eager to engage in political action for themselves. These men and women held a dizzying assortment of perspectives on how best to accomplish the emancipation of the slaves. At times, the tensions among the abolitionists proved impossible to ignore. As a result, the movement more than once split into competing organizations, each following its own strategy for achieving abolition.

One of the most obvious conflicts had to do with the question of gradual versus immediate emancipation. By the early 1830s, the movement was dominated by the so-called immediatists. Many antislavery advocates, however, still supported the concept of gradualism. "It would be cruelty, not kindness," preacher William Ellery Channing wrote in 1835, "to give [the slave] a freedom which he is unprepared to understand or enjoy."[64] Channing and others urged the immediatists to reconsider their position and lobby, instead, for gradual emancipation.

Following the publication of *Walker's Appeal*, though, the concept of gradualism had become unthinkable for the immediatists. Many of the more militant abolitionists charged that the gradualists were out of touch—or worse, not truly eager to help the slaves. William Lloyd Garrison was particularly pointed in his comments on the subject. "I utterly reject, as delusive and dangerous in the extreme," he wrote, "every plea which justifies a procrastinated [delayed] and an indefinite emancipation."[65] The war of words between the immediatists and the gradualists distracted members of both groups from the goal they shared.

Politics and Government

A second issue dividing the abolitionists had to do with politics and government. Some reformers emphatically discouraged abolitionists from allying themselves with political parties and goals. To these activists, politics was all about compromise. Thus, in seeking political solutions, abolitionists might compromise their own ideals as well. For William Lloyd Garrison, a strong advocate of this position, even voting represented unacceptable participation in government. In Garrison's opinion, in fact, it was better for Northerners to dissolve the Union than to coexist with Southerners. "No Union with Slaveholders,"[66] Garrison insisted time and time again; in fact, the statement soon became the editor's unofficial motto.

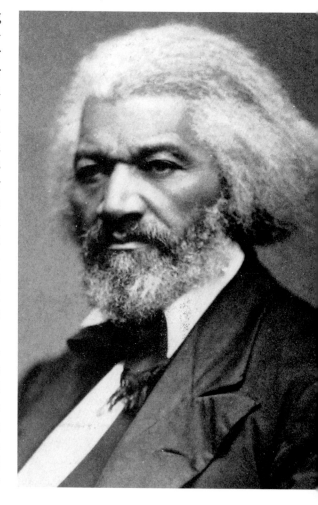

An escaped slave, Frederick Douglass was one of the abolitionist movement's most inspirational speakers.

Other abolitionists, however, rejected Garrison's views on politics. Many worked within the political system to find a governmental solution to the problem of slavery. In 1839, for example, several activists formed the Liberty

Party, an abolitionist organization that supported antislavery reformer James Birney for president in 1840 and 1844. Frederick Douglass argued that Garrison's doctrines might well keep the abolition movement free from any taint of cooperation with slavery, but would tend to strengthen slavery where it already existed. "My position," Douglass wrote, "is one of reform, not of revolution. I would act for the abolition of slavery through the Government—not over its ruins."[67]

Like the conflict between gradual and immediate emancipation, the question of politics split the abolition movement. Garrison and Douglass, in particular, had great difficulty putting aside their differences of opinion where political action was concerned. Despite the close personal connections that existed between them and their general agreement on nearly every other issue regarding slavery, they could not accept, or forgive, each other's stance on politics. A war of words ensued, and the men eventually stopped talking to each other altogether. So too did some of their most ardent supporters.

Some of the more neutral abolitionists tried their best to heal the breach. "In the name of the poor slave," one man begged Garrison, "let us cease quarreling, or seeming to quarrel, on the question of which of us has got hold of the best weapons of accomplishment."[68] In the end, Garrison and Douglass, along with their followers, were able to set aside their differences and join forces. Still, the squabble had driven a wedge between two valuable members of the movement, and the wounds never completely mended. Moreover, the controversy had taken time and energy that might have been used attacking slavery instead of other reformers.

More Quarrels

Other forces pushed the abolitionists apart, too. Black reformers, in particular, often felt ignored by their white colleagues. They pointed out that few blacks held positions of responsibility within the movement. The American Anti-Slavery Society, for instance, had twenty-six vice presidents at one point, none of whom were black. African American abolitionists also charged that their white counterparts were racists who had little interest in helping blacks who had gained their freedom. "They have overlooked the giant sin of prejudice," said black leader Theodore Wright. "They have passed by this foul monster, which is at once the parent and offspring of slavery."[69]

The question of violence was another divisive issue. David Walker had urged blacks to resist their masters, and a few later activists echoed his words. "You had better all die—*die immediately*," counseled black preacher Henry Highland Garnet, "than live as slaves."[70] Other reformers, however, objected to the use of violence. Not only did the idea repel many otherwise sympathetic Northerners; in the opinion of many abolitionists, it was simply wrong. "The slave cannot innocently adopt any and every expedient for vindicating his liberty," argued William Ellery Channing. "We owe a debt of humanity even to him who wrongs us."[71]

Abolitionists also did not agree about the role women should take in the antislavery movement. Most abolitionists had no difficulty with the notion that women should play some part in the movement, but the details of female involvement were hotly debated. Indeed, the question of whether women should be allowed to join the American Anti-Slavery Society (as William Lloyd Garrison advocated) or whether women should found a society of their own (as the wealthy New York abolitionist Lewis Tappan believed) helped split the society in 1840, severely damaging the organization's effectiveness.

The issue of abolition's connection with women's rights was also a subject of much debate. Some members of the movement noted that the position of women in American society was much like the position of slaves. These reformers joined forces with a small but growing movement for women's rights. Sojourner Truth and Sarah Grimké, among others, were equally active in both reform movements, and William Lloyd Garrison was one of several men eager to support women's rights in addition to working for abolition.

But many other abolitionists were reluctant to go along. A few reformers objected to the concept of women's rights in general. More often, though, opposition stemmed from questions of strategy. Dividing the efforts of the reformers between two different movements might divert attention from the goal of abolition, some abolitionists feared, and might turn away potentially sympathetic

Immediate Abolition

To modern audiences, the term "immediate abolition" seems clear enough. But in fact, different abolitionists meant somewhat different things when they used the phrase, especially during the early 1830s. To some, the phrase meant what one reformer, quoted in Gerda Lerner, *The Grimké Sisters from South Carolina*, described as "immediate emancipation gradually accomplished." By this, abolitionists meant immediate agreement from all parties that "slavery shall cease to exist—absolutely, unconditionally and irrevocably." Once this decision had been made, the actual emancipation of the slaves could take place more gradually. For people in this camp, the phrase therefore meant a position that differed from the traditional idea of gradual abolition only in the timing of the announcement.

That was the less common position. But even those who used the term in its literal meaning—to suggest that slaves should be freed that very day—did not generally suggest that the former slaves ought to be awarded the full rights of citizenship. "Immediate abolition," wrote William Lloyd Garrison, also quoted in Lerner's book, "does not mean that the slaves shall immediately exercise the right of suffrage [be allowed to vote], or be eligible to any office." Even the most radical of abolitionists typically agreed that such steps should be taken gradually. "It would [probably] not be judicious to invest emancipated slaves with the elective franchise," pointed out Lydia Maria Child, a staunch defender of African Americans, quoted in John Thomas, ed., *Slavery Attacked.* "Though it is not their fault that they have been kept brutally ignorant, it unfits them for voters."

audiences who disapproved of feminism. Moreover, as these activists saw it, the need for women's rights could not compare with the urgency of freeing the slaves. "Don't push your *women's* rights," advised Theodore Weld, "until *human* rights have gone ahead and broken the path."[72]

Disagreement and Strength

No one could doubt that the abolitionists were committed to their work and dedicated to the abolition of slavery. The trouble was not that they cared too little, but that they cared too much. Proud, stubborn, and contentious, the reformers had great difficulty accepting anyone else's ideas—even those of other reformers. As a result, the movement splintered again and again, often over issues that outsiders considered quite small, and angry words made healing difficult. Garrison, for one, wrote bitterly of allies "who have virtually abandoned our cause,"[73] and he was by no means the only reformer to take disagreement so personally.

The constant battles within the movement indeed weakened the cause of abolition and made it hard for reformers to speak with one voice. Still, on the whole, the diversity of opinion and personalities served the movement well. Despite the bickering, the ruptures, and the hostilities, the abolitionists of the pre–Civil War period accomplished a great deal. Through words and actions, through means political and moral, religious and governmental, they succeeded in drawing attention to the evils of slavery in a way their predecessors had never managed to do.

Chapter Five

Reaction to the Movement

Between 1830 and 1850, the abolitionists doggedly made their case again and again, to anyone who would listen—and to many who refused to hear. In the North, they made occasional converts, though not nearly as many as they might have wished. In the South, they made almost no headway at all. But though they had some trouble winning people to their cause, the abolitionists nonetheless had an impact on both North and South. The movement widened the gap between North and South, pushed slavery into the forefront of American political discussion, and set the stage for further conflict ahead. While the abolitionists' numbers were small, their effect was significant.

"An Unfortunate Legacy"

Before 1829, when the doctrine of gradual abolition prevailed among reformers, almost all abolitionists believed that slavery could be eliminated only with the support of Southern slaveholders. "Any plan of emancipation, to be effectual," wrote feminist and antislavery activist Frances Wright in 1825, "must consult at once the pecuniary [financial] interests and prevailing opinions of the southern planters."[74] Accordingly, gradualists often addressed their words specifically to the slaveholders of the

South. These activists begged, cajoled, and gently prodded the planters, trying to convince them that slavery was wrong—and economically inefficient.

At the time, there seemed to be good reasons to expect that Southerners might accept some form of emancipation. Early slaveholders such as Washington and Jefferson, after all, had questioned the morality of slavery, and their misgivings still lingered across the South. As historian Kenneth Stampp notes, it was common into the 1820s for slaveholders to talk of the institution as a "transitory evil [or] an unfortunate legacy of the past"[75] rather than as a positive good or a valued tradition. Southern interest in colonization schemes, too, suggested that many slaveholders would be pleased to see slavery disappear.

Moreover, the gradualists saw no realistic way to achieve their goal without Southern assistance. The country was divided evenly between free states and slave states, making it impossible for one side to accomplish much in Congress without the agreement of the other. The free states did not have the votes to abolish slavery by themselves. Unable to impose their own solution to the problem of slavery, the reformers of the Federal period had no alternative except to work with moderate Southerners.

Feminist and abolitionist Frances Wright believed that slavery could only be abolished with the support of slave owners.

A New Strategy
But with the rise in popularity of immediate abolition around 1830, the reformers reconsidered this strategy.

The *Amistad* Affair

—————————■—————————

In 1839, a Spanish ship called the *Amistad* left Havana, Cuba, with a cargo of African prisoners, all of whom had just been sold as slaves to two Cuban planters. But before the ship could reach the distant sugar plantations where the Africans would be put to work, a prisoner known as Joseph Cinque led his companions in a revolt. Taking over the *Amistad*, the African rebels eventually sailed the ship to Montauk, New York, where they were promptly arrested and jailed. Spain just as promptly demanded their return.

Within a week of the *Amistad*'s arrival, New England and New York abolitionists decided to make the case of Cinque and the other mutineers a focus of their efforts. In their opinion, it was unjust to doom Cinque and the rest to slavery. Spanish law, they pointed out, banned the importation of Africans into Cuba; thus the sale of the prisoners to the two Cuban planters was illegal. The abolitionists hoped that this case would make slavery real for thousands of otherwise apathetic Northerners, and to an extent it did exactly that. In the North, there was a great deal of public support for the mutineers. Some who sympathized with Cinque and his followers found themselves connecting the plight of these Africans with the hard-

David Walker, among others, had argued that it was immoral to ask the slaves to continue to wait until conditions were right for emancipation, and this line of reasoning had resonated with many Northern activists. At the same time, it was becoming increasingly apparent that the gradualists' goal of engaging Southern support was not working. Despite all the abolitionists' efforts, slavery was not withering away in the South. On the contrary, it was growing. Between 1800 and 1830, the slave population of the United States had more than doubled, to a total of nearly two million.

To be sure, a few Southern leaders still spoke up for colonization. "There are a number of slaveholders," argued a Virginia state legislator during a debate in 1832, "who would voluntarily surrender their slaves, if the State would provide the means of colonizing them elsewhere."[76] But by this time, it was clear to most observers that colonization was impractical. By 1830, after

ships and unfairness faced every day by the slaves of the South.

In the end, through the efforts of Lewis Tappan, John Quincy Adams, and other antislavery activists, Cinque and his followers won their case. "We may lament the dreadful acts by which [the Africans] asserted their liberty," ruled a Supreme Court justice, quoted in Charles Johnson and Patricia Smith, *Africans in America*, " . . . but there does not seem to us to be any ground for doubt that these Negroes ought to be deemed free." The Spanish claims were denied, and Cinque and the others were returned home to Africa. At the time, the *Amistad* affair ranked as one of the greatest victories the abolition movement had yet achieved.

A contemporary illustration depicts the revolt of the slaves onboard the *Amistad*.

fifteen years of hard work and enormous amounts of money, colonization advocates had succeeded in resettling only a few thousand blacks in West Africa. The logistics of transporting two million men, women, and children across the Atlantic seemed impossible.

To the more militant abolitionists who took the stage following the publication of *Walker's Appeal*, it seemed evident that Southerners had no real interest in eliminating slavery—and probably never intended to support emancipation to begin with. Southern leaders, the abolitionists charged, had only pretended to listen to the abolition forces. Even if no malice was involved, it was clear that the abolitionists' strategy had done nothing to move the South closer to emancipation. "We are told that the Southerners will of themselves [that is, on their own] do away with slavery," complained Lydia Maria Child. "But it is an obvious fact that all their measures have tended to perpetuate the system."[77]

As the post-1830 abolitionists saw it, they had two choices. They could continue their predecessors' gentle but ineffective attempts to change the hearts and minds of Southerners. Some gradualists did continue to follow this path, among them the moderate reformer William Ellery Channing, who in 1831 advocated that Northerners tell Southerners, "We consider slavery your calamity, not your crime; and we will share with you the burden of putting an end to it."[78] But most abolitionists of the time opted for an entirely new and different strategy. In essence, they chose to write off the South altogether. They expected no support from Southern whites, and they made little effort to obtain it. In their eyes, white Southerners were not the key to the solution; instead, they were the problem.

To be sure, some commentators had attacked slaveholders even before *Walker's Appeal*. George Bourne, a Presbyterian minister writing in 1816, had charged that since slavery and Christianity were incompatible, any slaveholder who claimed to be a Christian was "either an incurable Idiot . . . or an obdurate [stubborn] sinner."[79] But the insults became much more common as immediatism grew in popularity, and voices such as Channing's grew faint amid the increasingly militant comments of other activists. African American preacher Henry Highland Garnet referred to slaveholders as "guilty soul-thieves";[80] William Lloyd Garrison called them "patriotic hypocrites . . . [and] treasonable disunionists."[81] Far from working with the slaveholders, the new abolitionists seemed to be trying to outdo each other in hurling insults at the South.

The South Replies

The scathing language of these abolitionists was not meant to convert but to wound, and it did exactly that. White Southerners resented the words of Garrison, Garnet, and other reformers, and responded to them with bitterness and anger. It was one thing for Northerners to gently urge Southerners to give up slavery; it was quite another for abolitionists to charge all slaveholders with perpetuating a great evil. In the Southern view, the comments of antislavery Northerners represented a cruel betrayal of the South. "You have been making war upon us to our very hearthstones,"[82] charged planter James Henry Hammond of South Carolina.

Southerners quickly lashed back, using language of a kind that Douglass, Weld, and Garrison no doubt found familiar. Influential South Carolina politician John Calhoun described the abolitionists as "fanatical zealots" engaged in a "wicked and cruel"[83] quest against innocent Southerners. Other Southerners characterized the abolitionists as unthinking, misinformed, and ignorant. But whatever words they chose, most proslavery Southerners agreed that the new generation of antislavery activists needed to be taken seriously. These Northern reformers, Southerners were certain, presented a grave danger to the South.

In part, Southern slaveholders worried that Northern agitation might find some sympathy among Southern whites. Some parts of the South, such as the mountainous areas of Tennessee and Virginia, had few slaves, and

South Carolina politician John Calhoun condemned abolitionists as zealots out to destroy innocent Southerners.

the white residents of these areas already resented the powerful political influence of slaveholders. These regions, slaveholders feared, could eventually become abolitionist. The slaveowners of the South also worried that white Southerners too poor to have slaves of their own might be receptive to the antislavery message. Indeed, John Calhoun accused Northern reformers of trying to poison and corrupt Southern minds through relentless advocacy of antislavery doctrines.

But Southerners were particularly concerned about the abolitionists who advocated violence and slave rebellions. If literature such as *Walker's Appeal* reached the hands of Southern slaves, the planters reasoned, the result would certainly be disastrous. Many Southerners found it inconceivable that Northerners would allow documents of this sort to be published at all. Appalled by what Walker had written, for example, the mayor of Savannah, Georgia, requested that Boston officials destroy all existing copies of the *Appeal* and prevent publication of any more. (As Walker had broken no laws then in force in Massachusetts, the request was denied.)

In the two years following the publication of *Walker's Appeal*, the concern over violence was merely theoretical. But in August 1831, a Virginia slave named Nat Turner led a rebellion in which he and a few followers killed about sixty whites. Many Southerners immediately blamed the rebellion on abolitionist agitation, citing *Walker's Appeal* and William Lloyd Garrison's *The Liberator* as particular influences. The charges were probably not true—though Turner could read and write, there is no evidence that he ever encountered any antislavery documents—but they *could* have been true, and to Southern whites, that was what mattered. As the slaveholders saw it, abolitionists had caused Turner's rebel-

Virginian slaves rise up against their masters during Nat Turner's Rebellion in 1831. Turner and his followers succeeded in killing close to sixty whites.

lion, and if they were not stopped, they would encourage similar revolts all across the South.

In the wake of Turner's uprising, then, Southerners cracked down on abolitionists and their literature. Following the revolt, many Southern states banned all copies of the *The Liberator*, along with most other antislavery materials, and renewed their demands that Northern cities and states suppress these documents at their source. Rewards were posted for Garrison's arrest, and some slaveholders threatened the activists with more than just jail. "I warn all abolitionists, ignorant and infatuated barbarians as they are," wrote a furious James Henry Hammond, "that if chance shall throw any of them into our hands, they may expect a felon's death."[84]

The words of men like Hammond and Calhoun, of course, further inflamed the abolitionists. Antislavery activists charged that by demanding the suppression of abolitionist writings, Southerners were violating the reformers' basic civil rights. And slaveholders' threats of violence, the abolitionists pointed out, were inexcusable. To the activists, the words of these Southerners proved the abolitionists' case: There was, in fact, no reasoning with slaveholders, and there was no chance that Southerners would voluntarily abolish the institution of slavery.

Effects on the North

But of course, these antislavery activists were not really trying to win over the South. In attacking Southerners, the abolitionists' actual goal was to convince apathetic Northerners to take up the antislavery cause. The abolitionists hoped to make it unambiguously clear that slavery was brutal, evil, and sinful. Their ability to tell the truth about the slave system, these activists believed, was the movement's best asset. By agitating for immediate abolition, the reformers claimed the moral high ground in the debate.

Nor were the abolitionists sorry that their attacks infuriated the slaveholders. In the long run, the reformers believed, the sharp, angry responses of the Southerners would benefit the abolition movement. If slaveholders came across as hostile, out-of-touch, and intransigent, the people of the North would become disgusted—and would turn against slavery. Thus, many abolitionists were delighted to see Southerners use such heavy-handed tactics as trying to ban antislavery writings and threatening to arrest—even murder—Northerners who persisted in defending the rights of the slaves.

The reformers' strategy certainly converted some Northerners to the work of abolition. The tales of former slaves such as Frederick Douglass appalled and angered many who heard them. The hard-hitting works of Garrison, Child, the Grimké sisters, and others convinced many more. Theodore Weld's *American Slavery As It Is* became an immediate best seller. And some Northerners, alarmed by the Southern attacks on the cherished American institutions of free speech and a free press, supported the abolitionists based on a concern for civil rights.

Still, during the two decades that followed the publication of *Walker's Appeal*, the movement made relatively little headway

Sojourner Truth

One of the most intriguing of all the abolitionists was Sojourner Truth. Known early in her life as Isabella Van Wagener, Truth was born a slave in New York State about 1797; she won her freedom during the early 1800s as part of New York's gradual emancipation plan. Beginning in her childhood, Truth claimed to speak regularly with God, and she soon became an active preacher and evangelist. Taking the name Sojourner Truth (sojourner suggests "wanderer"), she began to travel across the country in 1843, giving talks wherever she went.

Truth soon became an important member of two separate but sometimes allied reform movements—abolition and women's rights. Her great value to both movements lay partly in her oratorical skills. Truth was by all accounts a compelling speaker, and few other reformers of the time rivaled her ability to excite an audience. (She often shared a speaker's platform with one of those few, Frederick Douglass.) But her importance also had to do with her absolute certainty, passed on to her audiences, that she was in contact with God. "Children, I talk to God and God talks to me!" was Truth's usual opening, quoted in Charles Van Doren, ed., *Webster's American Biographies*.

throughout the North. Few Northern citizens thought that slavery was a good system, and virtually none wished the institution reintroduced into their region. Nonetheless, most Northerners had no desire to interfere with slavery where it already existed. Indeed, economically, strategically, and racially, many Northerners believed that they had good cause to support Southern slavery, not to attack it.

Reasons for Opposition

For some, the economic argument against abolition was the most potent. Financially, North and South had become tightly connected by the 1830s. Goods flowed smoothly back and forth between the two regions, to the benefit of both. Many Northerners feared that abolitionist outrage might encourage the South to

Truth was a controversial figure. Like many abolitionists, she did not hesitate to say what she thought, which sometimes made

her a target of antireformist mobs. Her confident faith in a just and caring God also led her to disagree with other abolitionists on more than one occasion. "Frederick, is God dead?" she asked sharply of Frederick Douglass when he advocated violent resistance to slavery. After the Civil War, Truth worked tirelessly on behalf of freed slaves. She died in Michigan in 1883.

Freed slave Sojourner Truth traveled the country to promote her feminist and abolitionist ideologies.

cut these economic ties, to the detriment of Northern merchants and workers. "There are millions and millions of dollars which would be jeopardized by any rupture between North and South," one New York business leader told abolitionist Samuel May. "We cannot afford, sir, to let you and your associates succeed in your endeavor to overthrow slavery."[85]

Other Northerners rejected the abolitionists because of the movement's angry rhetoric, particularly its encouragement of violence by slaves against their white masters. Even many immediatists refused to advocate slave rebellions, and ordinary Northerners, generally apathetic toward the institution of slavery, were deeply troubled by the words of activists such as Walker and Garnet. A Boston newspaper, for example, termed *Walker's Appeal* "one of the most wicked and inflammatory productions that ever issued from the press."[86]

But even abolitionists who disapproved of slave violence were often considered too strident by Northerners. Francis Wayland, the president of Brown University, spoke for many when he charged that the abolitionists had adopted a "menacing and vindictive"[87] attitude toward slaveholders. According to these Northerners, this stance might well make Southerners ignore Northern ideas about slavery altogether. Without the steadying influence of the North, it was conceivable that Southerners would increase the brutality of slavery. As a group of Illinoisans asserted in 1837, slavery was "both injustice and bad policy," but the "promulgation of abolition doctrines tends rather to increase than to abate [stop] its evils."[88]

At the heart of Northern opposition to abolition, however, was racism. The great appeal of colonization schemes had been the removal of African Americans from the United States altogether. The abolitionists had had good reason to dismiss colonization as impractical, unfair, and ultimately unworkable, but the decision left them with the dilemma of what to do with the newly freed slaves. Few Northerners believed that all blacks would stay in the South. Instead, they feared, many emancipated slaves would move North, where they would move in next to white families and compete with white laborers for jobs. It was in the interest of many Northerners, then, to maintain slavery where it already existed.

Mobs and Violence

Antiabolitionist Northerners fought the reformers with words, using pamphlets, speeches, and newspapers to get their points across. When they could, they also barred the abolitionists from speaking in public. Many churches forbade visiting ministers to preach against slavery. Government officials often refused to allow antislavery lecturers to use public buildings for their talks. "Not a place can be found for love or money,"[89] lamented one activist when her abolitionist group proved unable to hold a meeting in Boston.

Those who opposed abolition also used violence and intimidation to keep the reformers from spreading their message. Theodore Weld routinely encountered hostile, angry audiences who tried to drown out his words with drums, whistles, and horns. Frederick Douglass was attacked by an angry crowd in Indiana, managing to escape with only a broken hand. In Boston, a vindictive mob—composed not only of street toughs but also of ordinary, middle-class citizens—threatened William Lloyd Garrison's life during an abolitionist convention. The mayor imprisoned Garrison for his own safety until the commotion died down.

A more tragic outcome befell a newspaper editor named Elijah Lovejoy. In 1833, Lovejoy began publishing an antislavery newspaper in St. Louis, Missouri, where slavery was legal. After three years of low circulation and general hostility from the local citizens, Lovejoy despaired of ever having his message heard. Accordingly, Lovejoy transferred his base of operations across the Mississippi River to the town of Alton, Illinois. In the free state of Illinois, Lovejoy expected to find a more tolerant and receptive community.

He was wrong. From the first, Lovejoy was the subject of repeated, angry attacks by the people of Alton. When his printing press arrived from St. Louis, a mob pushed it into the river, destroying it. An Ohio antislavery organization replaced the press for him, but another mob destroyed this one as well. For over a year, the cycle continued. Then, in November 1837, an Alton resident tried to set fire to a warehouse where the latest press was temporarily stored. Running into the street to stop the man, Lovejoy was gunned down by another citizen.

An antiabolitionist lynch mob attacks William Lloyd Garrison in Boston. Antiabolitionists often resorted to violence and intimidation to silence reformers.

News of Lovejoy's death stunned and appalled the abolitionists—and many ordinary Northerners as well. John Quincy Adams, a former president and no friend to slavery, said later that Lovejoy's murder created "a shock as of any earthquake throughout this continent."[90] To the abolitionists, the shooting of Lovejoy was a sobering reminder of the dangers they faced and the unpopularity of their cause, even among audiences who might have been expected to offer their support.

At the same time, though, Northern violence also emboldened the abolitionists. They had hoped that Southern attacks on the antislavery movement would disgust ordinary, reasonable Northerners and shake them out of their apathy, and to some degree, that had been the case. Now, they hoped that the angry behavior of the mobs would serve the same purpose. Questions of free speech and freedom of the press arose once again, this time in conjunction with the North rather than with the South. Recognizing the oppressive attempts to censor the abolitionists, some Northerners who did not necessarily approve of the activists' message nevertheless came to side with the antislavery movement for reasons of civil rights. As Weld put it, the people who disrupted his rallies had "mobbed up the cause vastly more than I could have lectured it up."[91]

Failure and Success

As 1850 approached, though, the abolition movement had not made many measurable gains. Although the abolitionists had done their best to paint slavery as evil, relatively few people had been persuaded to join the movement. Through the abolitionists' efforts, Southerners had only come to hate and distrust the anti-slavery cause and, increasingly, to hate and distrust the North in general. Even within the North, abolitionism was controversial at best and detestable at worst. True, there had been converts to the cause, many of whom had become enthusiastic advocates for abolition. Nonetheless, slavery was as strong as ever, and in 1850 there was no evidence that the abolitionists had helped in any way to ease the burdens of the slaves.

Yet the abolitionists persisted. During the twenty years since the publication of *Walker's Appeal*, they had lobbied constantly for their cause, and they meant to continue. And in fact, the

"Insult, Outrage, Suffering . . . Even Death"

———————◼———————

Between 1830 and 1850, the abolitionists complained frequently about the unwillingness of Northerners to accept the antislavery message. These complaints were genuine and heartfelt. However, the abolitionists were a contrary bunch of people, and it is fair to say that some abolitionists relished being in the minority. That was particularly true of William Lloyd Garrison, who actually seemed to delight in taking on the role of unpopular gadfly. He enjoyed the notoriety his statements brought him, and he halfway hoped for increasingly violent responses from the people of the North. As quoted in William E. Cain, ed., *William Lloyd Garrison and the Fight Against Slavery*, Garrison cheerfully advised his supporters at one point that taking up the cause of abolition "may subject us to insult, outrage, suffering, yea, even death itself." One historian, quoted in Richard O. Curry, *The Abolitionists*, argues that Garrison's life "would probably have been spent in protesting even if slavery had never existed," and there is plenty of evidence to support this view. Certainly, Garrison's enthusiasm for protest and reform made him an extremely dedicated abolitionist.

activists had accomplished much more than they knew. They had brought slavery to the forefront of American political discussion; they had raised the issue and refused to remain silent about it. Within the next ten years, sparked in large part by the untiring efforts of the abolitionists, the controversy over slavery in the United States would change dramatically. Hard as it would have been for most people to believe in 1850, within just fifteen years American slavery would be no more.

Chapter Six

Distrust, Disunion, and War

From the vantage point of the early 1830s, the abolitionists had thought their task was simple. To win the support of Northerners, they thought, it was only necessary to call Southern slavery what it was: a sin against humanity and a crime against nature. In their view, many ordinary Northerners would join the cause once they knew the truth about slavery. These citizens, in turn, would demand that their leaders do whatever was necessary to eradicate the institution. "You and I will continue to cry 'woe, woe, woe,'" abolitionist Samuel May told William Lloyd Garrison in 1831, "until the [leaders] in the land are roused to answer the demand of the people."[92]

Like other antislavery activists, both May and Garrison assumed, or, at least, hoped, that this time would come quickly. They were wrong, of course; twenty, even twenty-five years after this conversation, May and Garrison were still crying "woe." But in the end, it was not so much that the reformers' message was wrong, but that the time was not yet right. The efforts of the abolitionists alone could not eliminate slavery as practiced in the United States. But political changes could—and did. Beginning around 1850, a string of political events altered the way that Northerners thought about the Southern states and the institution

Plumes of smoke billow from a factory in Boston. Since colonial times, manufacturing had played an ever increasing role in the economy of the North.

of slavery itself. These changes finally enabled the abolitionists' message to find fertile ground within the North.

Sectional Differences

Ever since the inception of the United States, slavery had represented the main division in American political life. Legal in the South and forbidden in the North, the institution summed up the distinctions between the two regions. That was reflected in the very language Americans used. By 1850, the terms "slave states" and "free states" had become synonymous with "South" and "North" and were familiar to every American.

In fact, all the major differences between the two regions were shaped by the question of slavery. For instance, the South had remained largely agricultural and rural because slave labor was most useful on farms, while Northerners had begun to industrialize and urbanize. By 1850, just eight of the nation's fifty largest cities were in slave territory, and most of the country's industrial output came from the North. Another difference was immigration. Most immigrants from Europe headed to the North rather than to the South, since there was little need for cheap labor where slave labor was available. As a result, the Southern white population remained predominantly unchanged, while the white population of the North became increasingly diverse. These differences led to political hostility and misunderstandings between the two regions.

A Spirit of Compromise

The divisions created by slavery placed the United States in a delicate position. Split roughly in half between slave states and free states since its beginnings, the new nation moved carefully where slavery was concerned. In hopes of keeping their new nation unified and strong, leaders in both sections adopted a spirit of compromise on slavery. The two sides agreed to disagree. The country would thus remain half slave and half free until such time as

A group of slaves harvests cotton on a Southern plantation. The economy of the pre-Civil War South was largely agricultural and dependent on slave labor.

Proslavery Arguments

■

As slavery increasingly came under attack by the abolition movement, the defenders of the institution developed several arguments to demonstrate that slavery was good. Some thinkers repeated the historical and biblical rationales used to justify slavery during the colonial period. Southerners soon agreed, in particular, that every great culture had relied on slave labor. "Such a class you must have," argued James Henry Hammond, quoted in Eric McKitrick, ed., *Slavery Defended*, "or you would not have that other class which leads progress, civilization, and refinement."

In defending slavery, Southerners also tried to refute the arguments of Northerners who attacked it. Many slaveholders, for instance, asserted that Northern white laborers were not treated any better than slaves. This touched a sensitive spot for many abolitionists, who saw an enormous difference in status between an impoverished slave and an impoverished free laborer, but who had to admit that materially the two groups were often difficult to distinguish. Similarly, slaveholders denied that Southern slavery was as brutal as the abolitionists reported. "The slaves are all well fed," declared George Fitzhugh in his *Sociology for the South*, "well clad, have plenty of fuel, and are happy."

Fundamentally, the slaveholders believed that slavery was the natural status of blacks. Africans were an inferior people, both morally and intellectually, Southerners explained, and slavery protected and uplifted them. "The black race of Central Africa . . . came among us in a low, degraded, and savage condition," wrote John Calhoun, quoted in McKitrick's *Slavery Defended*, "and in the course of a few generations it has grown up under the fostering care of our institutions . . . to its present comparatively civilized condition." In this view, enslaving blacks was not at all cruel, but benevolent—and necessary as well.

the South decided to eliminate slavery (or, less likely, the North chose to permit slaveholding once again). In the meantime, questions that arose around slavery would be settled in a way that satisfied both sections.

For many years, then, compromise was possible. But around

1830, with the growth of abolitionist agitation, the situation began to change. As abolitionists increasingly adopted the position that slavery was evil, slaveholders, in turn, stopped apologizing for their institution. Instead, Southerners began to argue that slavery was moral, just, and beneficial to planter and slave alike. Influential thinkers such as John Calhoun and James Henry Hammond insisted that Southerners had no reason to be embarrassed by slavery; instead, they argued, it should be a source of regional pride.

Economic realities played a role in this shift in Southern opinion. "The South had become a cotton empire," observes historian Bruce Catton, "and slavery looked like an absolutely essential element in Southern prosperity."[93] But abolitionist pressure also played a role in the change of thinking. It was no coincidence that the new Southern attitude arose just as abolitionists were beginning to organize. With slavery suddenly under attack, Southern leaders fought back by defending it. "The Abolitionists assailed us," wrote proslavery essayist George Fitzhugh, explaining the change in thinking. "[W]e looked more closely into our circumstances; [and] became satisfied that slavery was morally right."[94]

While compromise became more difficult during the 1830s, it was not yet impossible. Leaders on both sides continued to work to find common ground. Few Southerners during this time ignored Northern concerns altogether; few Northerners subscribed to William Lloyd Garrison's principle of avoiding negotiation with the South. But, by 1850, the earlier spirit of compromise had very nearly dissolved. The rise of the abolitionists—and of the radical defenders of slavery, sometimes known as the "fire-eaters"—had increased the tension between the two regions. Given the angry rhetoric, the strong accusations, and the sheer stubbornness exhibited by radicals on both sides, coming to any kind of agreement on slavery was rapidly becoming harder.

Slave Power

From the point of view of the abolitionists, the main fault lay with the South, and there was certainly some truth to that perspective. Between 1830 and 1850, Southern leaders placed continual demands on Northerners with regard to slavery. Sparked in large part by the attacks of the abolitionists, Southerners, led by the fire-eaters, not only demanded that Northerners suppress the writings and speeches of the activists, but increasingly insisted that the North remain silent on the topic of slavery. As John Calhoun proclaimed in an 1838 speech, any Northern attempt to describe slavery as immoral would constitute "a direct and dangerous attack on the institutions of all the slaveholding States."[95]

What the abolitionists most resented, however, was not the truculent attitude of Calhoun and other Southerners, but the willingness of Northerners to accede to Southern demands. While the South was growing bolder and more radical, it seemed that the North was becoming more timid and submissive. In the interests of maintaining harmony between the regions, the abolitionists charged, too many Northerners were content to make concessions. Northern voters, mourned abolitionist James Birney in 1840, were "bowing the knee to the dark spirit of Slavery."[96]

To the abolitionists, the stakes were high. The reformers feared that Southerners, if they were not stopped, would eventually come to dominate the government. Indeed, many abolitionists believed that this was the ultimate intention of men like Calhoun. Members of the antislavery movement spoke bitterly of what they called slave power or slaveocracy, by which they meant the Southern desire to spread its institutions and its way of life across the country. The South's entire political strategy, wrote Lydia Maria Child, "has been framed for the preservation and extension of slave power."[97]

But despite the warnings of the reformers, nothing seemed to shake the North out of its apathy—not the abolitionists' constant recitation of the brutality of slavery nor their warnings about the political goals of slavery's defenders. Discouraged but not defeated, the abolitionists refused to give up. Through the 1830s and most of the 1840s, they continued to press their agenda, hoping that someday their message would be heard by the great mass of Northerners.

Slavery in the Territories

What finally roused the North was not the issue of slavery in the South, but the question of slavery in the western territories. According to an 1820 Congressional agreement known as the Missouri Compromise, one of the first attempts to address the

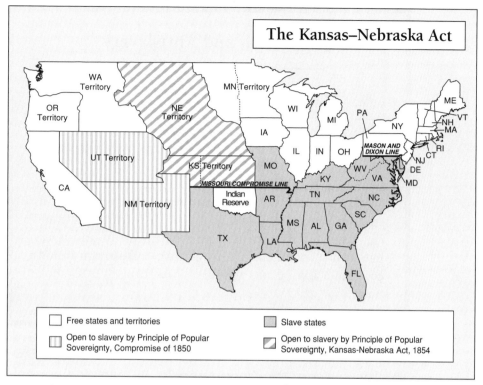

The Kansas–Nebraska Act

Free states and territories

Slave states

Open to slavery by Principle of Popular Sovereignty, Compromise of 1850

Open to slavery by Principle of Popular Sovereignty, Kansas-Nebraska Act, 1854

issue, slavery was to be permitted in the Arkansas Territory south of Missouri; the institution was to be banned, however, in all other territories then held by the United States, including most of the Great Plains and part of the northern Rockies. Though passing the Missouri Compromise had been difficult, the deal was more or less acceptable to both Northerners and Southerners.

But in the late 1840s, the delicate balance of the Missouri Compromise came under attack. In 1848, when the United States acquired most of the modern day Southwest following a war with Mexico, Southern leaders insisted that the region be opened to slavery. Lawmakers eventually settled the issue by passing the Compromise of 1850, according to which California would enter the Union as a free state and the question of slavery in the rest of the territory would be deferred indefinitely. Southern insistence in opening the new territories to slavery, however, worried abolitionists—and other Northerners as well. It seemed that Southerners were intent on changing the rules.

Their fear was well-founded. In 1854, Southern lawmakers, with the help of a few Northern colleagues, pushed a bill through

Abolition and Antislavery

—————————◼—————————

The words *abolition* and *antislavery*, though similar, did not have precisely the same meanings during the 1850s. Supporters of abolition believed that slavery should be eliminated everywhere in America. People who called themselves antislavery, in contrast, were concerned mainly with the spread of slavery into the territories. All abolitionists were antislavery, but it was possible to hold antislavery positions and not be an abolitionist. Both the Republican Party and the Free-Soil movement were fundamentally antislavery rather than abolitionist, although each organization included quite a few people who described themselves as abolitionists.

Congress that completely invalidated the Missouri Compromise. This law, known as the Kansas-Nebraska Act, allowed the people of each territory to vote on whether to allow slavery or not. Then, in 1857, the Supreme Court, deciding a case involving a slave named Dred Scott, went even further. Scott, a slave from Missouri, had spent parts of twelve years living with his master in Illinois and Wisconsin; he sued for his freedom on the grounds that those two regions did not permit slavery. The Supreme Court not only decided that Scott would remain a slave, but ruled, additionally, that Congress had no authority to limit slavery in any territories at all.

Southerners cheered both the Kansas-Nebraska Act and the *Dred Scott* decision. Abolitionists, however, were livid. "Are we to accept, without question, these new readings of the Constitution?" demanded abolitionist William Cullen Bryant. "Never! Never!"[98] More important, even Northerners who did not oppose slavery were furious. "There is such a thing as the SLAVE POWER," editorialized one conservative Cincinnati newspaper following the *Dred Scott* case. "It has marched over and annihilated the boundaries of the states. We are now one homogeneous slaveholding community."[99]

The Fugitive Slave Law

To Northerners, the opening of territories to slavery was not the only warning that Southerners were beginning to dictate national policy. Another case in point was the Fugitive Slave Law. Part of the Compromise of 1850, this law demanded that Northerners arrest and return any escaped slaves who reached the North and called for fines and prison sentences for those who disobeyed. The abolitionists despised this law. Many vowed not to comply with its provisions; some promised to meet it with violence. "If any man approaches [my] house in search of a slave," proclaimed black activist Martin Delany, "[h]e cannot enter that house and we both live."[100]

Once again, the abolitionists were joined by other Northerners. "The Fugitive Slave Bill has especially been of service to the anti-slavery movement,"[101] wrote Frederick Douglass, and he was right. Thousands of Northerners with no previous antipathy toward slavery were outraged by the passage of the act, and like the abolitionists they resolved to resist it whatever the cost. Nearly all Northern states passed "personal liberty" laws designed to interfere with the carrying out of the Fugitive Slave Act. In several well-publicized cases, angry mobs of Northerners even stormed courthouses and prisons to set arrested slaves free.

The stakes, once again, were high. Slave power was clearly a reality, and no one knew when—or whether—Southerners would be satisfied with their gains. For all Northerners knew, the slaveholders would next petition to establish slavery in Michigan, say, or force it back into New Hampshire. "The South will claim that the master has a right to take his Slaves into a free State," predicted abolitionist Theodore Parker, "first, for a definite time, say seven years; next, for an indefinite period in perpetuity."[102]

Suddenly and unexpectedly, the abolitionists were close to the mainstream of Northern opinion. Increasingly suspicious of Southerners and their intentions, ordinary Northerners were growing more hostile to the South. True, most Northerners had not completely caught up to the abolitionists. Even after the *Dred Scott* decision in 1857, few Northerners were eager to eliminate slavery in the states where it already existed. Still, the changes were real. The abolitionists no longer seemed unrealistic and out of touch. "Extremes are getting less extreme," wrote one abolitionist, noting that even the most radical members of the movement "are [now] listened to with some respect."[103]

Politics, Novels, and Violence

Northerners responded in several different ways to the apparent threat posed by the South. The Free-Soil political party, devoted to keeping slavery out of the territories, sprang up in 1848. "We inscribe on our banner 'Free Soil, Free Speech, Free Labor, and Free Men,'" read the party's platform, "and under it will fight on, and fight ever."[104] The Free-Soil movement was soon replaced by a similar organization, the Republican Party. Both the Republicans and the Free-Soilers included abolitionists, some of whom had been active in the now-defunct Liberty Party earlier in the 1840s, but both parties were fundamentally against the spread of slave power rather than against slavery itself.

Abolitionists also kept up the pressure against slavery and slaveholders. In 1852, Harriet Beecher Stowe published the anti-slavery novel *Uncle Tom's Cabin*. One of the most popular books of its time, the novel attracted enormous attention both in the North and in the South. Slaveholders screamed that the book was inaccurate and unfair; one Southern magazine editor, commissioning a review of the novel, instructed his reviewer to write an article that would be "as hot as hell fire, blasting and searing the reputation of the vile wretch in petticoats who could write such a volume."[105] Northerners, on the other hand, loved it; they wept at the cruelty of the slaveholders and applauded the courage of the slaves who were the subjects of the book.

But politics and words were not the only ways in which anti-slavery sentiment expressed itself during the 1850s. In 1859, a white abolitionist named John Brown, leading an armed group of twenty-one followers, seized a federal arsenal at Harpers Ferry, Virginia (now West Virginia). Brown's intention was to distribute the weapons in the arsenal among local slaves, enabling them to shoot their way to freedom. From the beginning, however, the odds were strongly against him and his small band of supporters. After a shootout with federal agents, Brown was captured, tried, and executed.

Brown's attack was a complete failure; not a single slave had been freed. But the impact of the raid was enormous. To Southerners, the attack was a symbol of the lengths to which abolitionists would go to eradicate slavery. To the abolitionists, though—and to an increasing number of other Northerners as well—John Brown was a martyr. Even many who disapproved of Brown's actions could sympathize with the motive behind them. "Let every man work for the abolition of slavery in his own way," said Frederick Douglass. "I would help all and hinder none."[106]

Secession and War

Brown's raid very nearly put an end to cooperation and understanding between North and South, and what little trust remained vanished after the 1860 presidential election. That year, Illinois Republican Abraham Lincoln won a bitterly contested election, with nearly all his votes coming from Northerners. Lincoln freely admitted his distaste for slavery and his determination to keep the institution out of the territories. However, he also stated unequivocally that he would not eliminate slavery in the South. "I have no lawful right to do so," he said more than once, "and I have no inclination to do so."[107]

Federal soldiers lead John Brown to the gallows in December 1859. Earlier that year, Brown led twenty-one abolitionists on a raid of the arsenal at Harpers Ferry, Virginia.

Bleeding Kansas

In 1855, soon after the passage of the Kansas-Nebraska Act, a bitter struggle broke out in Kansas between Southern defenders of slavery and Northern members of the Free-Soil movement—a group that included many abolitionists. Given that Congress had allowed the people of each territory to decide about slavery for themselves, people on both sides were determined to gain control. Pro- and antislavery forces burned houses, stole horses, and threatened each other with violence. One group of Southern sympathizers destroyed the Free-Soil town of Lawrence. In response, a vigilante group led by John Brown—the same John Brown who later became famous for his raid on the arsenal at Harpers Ferry—ambushed and killed five proslavery men. The struggles in Kansas presaged the Civil War, not only in the violence used by both sides but by the conviction among many people in both North and South that the bloodshed was justified.

In 1858 a group of armed slaveowners on horseback fires upon abolitionist settlers in Kansas.

These assurances, though, were not enough for the South. In the wake of Lincoln's election, several Southern states announced their intention to secede from the Union. These states quickly banded together to form a new government and a new nation, the Confederate States of America. The new nation was set up along the same principles as the old, with one important exception. The right to own slaves would be guaranteed—indeed, it would be written into the Confederacy's constitution.

If the Confederate states succeeded in their quest for independence, the Union would be broken. The new United States, in that case, would consist of the free states together with whatever slave states chose to remain loyal to Lincoln's government. Many Northerners found the prospect of a divided nation unacceptable. Abraham Lincoln quickly made it clear not only that he would refuse to recognize the Confederacy, but that he would go to war to preserve the Union. In the spring of 1861, the Civil War began.

Both sides believed that the war would be short. Both sides were very, very wrong. Month after bloody month, the two sides fought. Armies clashed at Antietam in Maryland, Bull Run in Virginia, Shiloh in Tennessee. Hundreds of thousands of soldiers lost their lives in these battles; many more died of disease, hunger, and exhaustion. At times it seemed that the South was winning; at other times, it was apparent that the advantage belonged to the North. The South had perhaps the greater determination, but the North had more soldiers, more supplies, and better transportation and industry to support the needs of the army. In the end, the war would last four bitter years before the Union finally prevailed.

War and the Abolitionists

The outbreak of war delighted most abolitionists. Finally, the North had stood firm against the spreading slaveocracy, and a Northern victory seemed likely to end in abolition at last. "The election of Mr. Lincoln was a judgment against Slavery,"[108] crowed Massachusetts senator Charles Sumner. Even William Lloyd Garrison, a staunch pacifist who generally rejected political solutions, did not complain. As historian Henry Mayer puts it, the political changes of the previous few years had convinced Garrison that Lincoln and the Republicans might actually be "history's vehicle, the train that would at last pull the abolition car into the station."[109]

Not all abolitionists were willing to give Lincoln their complete trust. Black abolitionists, in particular, noted that whatever his other virtues, the president was a racist. "There must be the position of superior and inferior," Lincoln said at one point, "and I . . . am in favor of having the superior position assigned to the white race."[110] Moreover, Lincoln initially cast the war as a struggle for the Union rather than as a battle against slavery. Some abolitionists, white and black alike, feared that Lincoln might restore the Union by leaving slavery intact throughout the South—a compromise that these reformers found intolerable.

But by late 1862, Lincoln had dismissed the option of compromise. It had become clear to him that slavery was at the root of the discord between North and South. To restore the Union without eliminating slavery would simply put off the inevitable day of reckoning. In September 1862, as a result, Lincoln issued the Emancipation Proclamation, a document that declared the end of slavery in rebel territory. As of January 1, 1863, the proclamation announced, all slaves in these regions would be "then, thenceforward, and forever free."[111]

Technically, the Emancipation Proclamation had no immediate legal force. Lincoln, of course, had no power to enforce the edict in the parts of the South where the Confederacy still held sway. And since he was unwilling to face the wrath of slaveholders in the loyal border states and in the areas of the South already recaptured by the Union, Lincoln specifically left these regions out of the proclamation. But even if the Emancipation Proclamation did not actually free a single slave, it was important for what it implied. For the first time, the government had issued a document that declared that slavery was wrong. The position of the U.S. government was now clear. If and when the North won the war, slavery *would* be banned.

The abolitionists, not surprisingly, were thrilled with the Emancipation Proclamation. Throughout the North, write historians James Oliver Horton and Lois E. Horton, African Americans "broke into wild celebration" on New Year's Day of 1863, "greeting [the proclamation] with singing, dancing, prayers, lofty rhetoric, and plain speaking about friends and relatives still in slavery."[112] William Lloyd Garrison used capital letters to express his sentiments, "THREE MILLIONS OF SLAVES SET FREE!" read the headline in the next edition of *The Liberator.* (Garrison's numbers were sightly off; there were actually about four million slaves at the time.) "GLORY HALLELUJAH!"[113]

In this illustration, Abraham Lincoln reads the Emancipation Proclamation to his cabinet. The proclamation made it clear that a Union victory would result in the freeing of the slaves.

In April 1865, the war ended in a Union victory. All across the South, Union soldiers—and occasionally, masters—gathered slaves together and told them that their bondage was over. "Such rejoicing and shouting you never heard in your life,"[114] Virginia slave Fannie Berry recalled many decades later. The passage of the Thirteenth Amendment to the U.S. Constitution in December 1865 put into law what everyone already knew: slavery would be outlawed forever. "Neither slavery nor involuntary servitude," the amendment read, " . . . shall exist within the United States, or any place subject to their jurisdiction."[115]

The abolitionists had been working for years toward a Thirteenth Amendment, and now, their greatest dream had come true. The slave system, with its brutality and inhumanity, was no more. "Old things are passing away," mused black abolitionist Robert Purvis halfway through the war, anticipating the magnitude of the changes that were to come. "All things are becoming new. Now a black man has rights, under this government, which every white man, here and everywhere, is bound to respect."[116] The forces of justice, at last, had triumphed.

Afterward

The passage of the Thirteenth Amendment marked the end of slavery in the United States. For two centuries, the laws of the slave states had systematically beaten down African Americans, oppressed them and deprived them of their rights; now, four million African Americans were free. In theory, at least, they could go where they pleased, provide for themselves as they saw fit, and live without fear of threat and punishment. The change was momentous, and the abolitionists could celebrate not only the achievement but also their role in bringing the era of slavery to a close.

After the war, the victorious North established a plan to bring the seceding Southern states back into the Union as quickly and peacefully as possible. Since this plan entailed the rebuilding of both the South and the Union itself, this period was known as the era of Reconstruction. During these years, federal troops took charge of the South, and military governments were set up in the former slave states. The troops were there largely to maintain order while Southerners reestablished their state governments to the satisfaction of Union leaders. But the soldiers had another purpose as well: to safeguard the rights of the newly freed slaves.

The reforms of the Reconstruction period were many. Schools were established for the former slaves, adults as well as children. An organization called the Freedmen's Bureau, created by Congress before the end of the Civil War, provided food, clothing, and other basic supplies for freed slaves. And the passage of the Fourteenth and Fifteenth Amendments to the Constitution, in 1866 and 1869, respectively, guaranteed citizenship and voting rights for black men. (Women, black and white, had to wait for the Nineteenth Amendment to obtain these rights.) During these years, Southern voters even elected several blacks to Congress.

The work of Reconstruction was accomplished, in part, by some of the most prominent abolitionists of the prewar period. Frederick Douglass, in particular, labored tirelessly on behalf of the Southern blacks, working most notably to safeguard the right of African American men to vote. Lydia Maria Child continued to lobby for racial tolerance; Sojourner Truth urged the government to offer former slaves farmland in Kansas and elsewhere on the Great Plains. Thaddeus Stevens, a white Pennsylvania congressman who had been active in the fight for emancipation, drafted the Fourteenth Amendment and fought tirelessly for its enforcement.

"The Voice of Conscience"

Unfortunately, the gains of Reconstruction did not last. By 1877, the federal government had relaxed its grip on the South. White Southerners elected Confederate war heroes and officials to Congress and state legislatures and set out to suppress the hard-earned rights of the former slaves. Racial prejudice ran rampant throughout the South; hate groups such as the Ku Klux Klan sprang up to terrorize and injure blacks who tried to attend schools, vote in elections, or even move freely through their hometowns. Segregation, or the enforced separation of the races, became the law throughout the South—and in much of the North as well.

Indeed, following the end of Reconstruction, most Southern blacks lived in circumstances not far removed from those of slavery. Southern states established "black codes" that usually kept blacks from voting, sometimes prohibited them from owning land of their own, and often forced them to work for a particular landowner. As historians Allan Nevins and Henry Steele Commager put it, these laws were "designed to 'keep the Negro in his place,' which was, of course, a subordinate one."[117] Though the

In 1865 a large crowd of blacks in Washington, D.C., celebrates the passage of the Thirteenth Amendment, which marked the end of slavery in the United States.

African Americans of the South were free, they were free in name only. Not until the civil rights movement took shape during the 1950s and 1960s did the situation begin to improve.

Still, the appalling treatment Southern blacks received after Reconstruction does not take away from the remarkable work done by the abolitionists. Against great odds, the men and women who formed the abolitionist movement had helped to eliminate slavery—and aided in amending the U.S. Constitution to prevent the institution from ever returning. Again and again, they argued that slavery was both a sin and a disgrace and that the only remedy was to set the slaves free. And despite taunts, threats, and physical attacks, members of the movement never changed their course or compromised their cause. "It was a duty to fulfil this task," wrote Lydia Maria Child, "and worldly considerations should never stifle the voice of conscience."[118]

The word "conscience" was well-chosen, for the abolitionist movement served in large part as the conscience of the nation. Whether their message was accepted or ignored, whether they were greeted with acceptance or hostility, the abolitionists bore witness against the institution of slavery. They reminded Americans that the nation could do better. They pointed out the contradictions between the institution of slavery and the moral and religious principles on which the country was founded; they urged the people of the United States to follow high standards of ethical conduct. They argued, simply, for Americans to do what was right, whether Americans wanted to do it or not. Their words, their methods, and their essential message would be echoed in other social reform movements throughout American history.

Notes

Introduction: The Abolitionists

1. Quoted in Henry Mayer, *All on Fire: William Lloyd Garrison and the Abolition of Slavery.* New York: St. Martin's, 1998, p. 119.
2. Quoted in Mason Lowance, ed., *Against Slavery: An Abolitionist Reader.* New York: Penguin, 2000, p. 41.
3. Bruce Catton, *The Civil War.* Originally published 1960; reprint, Boston: Houghton Mifflin, 1987, p. 10.

Chapter One: Slavery in America

4. Quoted in Eugene Genovese, *Roll, Jordan, Roll: The World the Slaves Made.* New York: Vintage, 1976, p. 30.
5. Quoted in Genovese, *Roll, Jordan, Roll*, p. 29.
6. Quoted in Charles Johnson and Patricia Smith, *Africans in America.* New York: Harcourt Brace, 1998, p. 48.
7. Quoted in Lydia Maria Child, *An Appeal in Favor of That Class of Americans Called Africans.* Originally published 1836; reprint, New York: Arno Press, 1968, p. 42.
8. Quoted in B.A. Botkin, ed., *Lay My Burden Down.* Chicago: University of Chicago Press, 1945, p. 120.
9. Quoted in Kenneth Stampp, *The Peculiar Institution.* New York: Alfred A. Knopf, 1967, p. 171.
10. Quoted in Botkin, *Lay My Burden Down*, p. 183.

11. Quoted in Genovese, *Roll, Jordan, Roll*, p. 66.
12. Quoted in Theodore Weld, *American Slavery As It Is: Testimony of a Thousand Witnesses.* Originally published 1839; reprint, Salem, NH: Ayer, 1991, p. 73.
13. Quoted in Stampp, *The Peculiar Institution*, p. 146.
14. Quoted in Botkin, *Lay My Burden Down*, pp. 75–76.
15. Quoted in Harvey Wish, ed., *Slavery in the South.* New York: Farrar, Straus, 1964, p. 77.
16. Quoted in Botkin, *Lay My Burden Down*, p. 120.
17. Quoted in Wish, *Slavery in the South*, p. 76.
18. Quoted in Gilbert Osofsky, ed., *Puttin' on Ole Massa.* New York: Harper and Row, 1969, p. 317.
19. Quoted in Weld, *American Slavery As It Is*, p. 42.
20. Quoted in Stanley Feldstein, *Once a Slave: The Slave's View of Slavery.* New York: William Morrow, 1971, p. 60.

Chapter Two: Colonial Abolitionists

21. Quoted in George H. Moore, ed., *Notes on the History of Slavery in Massachusetts.* New York: D. Appleton, 1866, no page number available.

22. Quoted in Susanne Everett, *History of Slavery.* Edison, NJ: Chartwell, 1996, p. 134.

23. George Keith, *An Exhortation & Caution to Friends Concerning Buying or Keeping of Negroes.* New York: William Bradford, 1693, no page number available.

24. Quoted in Lowance, *Against Slavery*, p. 22.

25. Keith, *An Exhortation & Caution to Friends*, no page number available.

26. Samuel Sewall, *The Selling of Joseph: A Memorial.* Boston: Samuel Sewall, 1700, no page number available.

27. Quoted in Lowance, *Against Slavery*, p. 13.

28. Sewall, *Selling of Joseph*, no page number available.

29. Quoted in Allen D. Candler, *The Colonial Records of the State of Georgia: Proceedings and Minutes of the Governor and Council from Aug. 6, 1771–Feb. 13, 1782.* Atlanta: Franklin Turner, 1907, no page number available.

30. Quoted in Robin D.G. Kelley and Earl Lewis, *To Make Our World Anew: A History of Black Americans.* New York: Oxford University Press, 2000, p. 109.

31. Quoted in John W. Wright, ed., The New York Times *Almanac 2005.* New York: Penguin, 2005, p. 58.

32. Quoted in James Oliver Horton and Lois E. Horton, *Hard Road to Freedom.* New Brunswick, NJ: Rutgers University Press, 2001, p. 64.

33. Quoted in Johnson and Smith, *Africans in America*, pp. 202–203.

Chapter Three:
The Rise of a New Movement

34. Quoted in Lowance, *Against Slavery*, p. 132.

35. David Walker, *David Walker's Appeal*, ed. Charles M. Wiltse. Originally published 1829 under the title *Appeal to the Coloured Citizens of the World;* reprint, New York: Hill and Wang, 1965, p. 75.

36. Walker, *David Walker's Appeal*, p. 16.

37. Walker, *David Walker's Appeal*, p. 26.

38. Quoted in Johnson and Smith, *Africans in America*, p. 343.

39. Walker, *David Walker's Appeal*, p. 76.

40. Quoted in Richard O. Curry, *The Abolitionists: Reformers or Fanatics?* New York: Holt, Rinehart and Winston, 1965, p. 84.

41. Walker, *David Walker's Appeal*, p. 69.

42. Walker, *David Walker's Appeal*, p. 55.

43. Quoted in Lowance, *Against Slavery*, p. 25.

44. Quoted in Mayer, *All on Fire*, p. 112.

45. Weld, *American Slavery As It Is,* p. 7.

46. Quoted in John L. Thomas, ed., *Slavery Attacked.* Englewood Cliffs, NJ: Prentice-Hall, 1965, p. 104.

47. Quoted in Lowance, *Against Slavery*, p. 206.

48. Quoted in Mayer, *All on Fire*, p. 112.

Chapter Four:
One Cause, Many Voices

49. George Fitzhugh, *Sociology for the South.* Richmond, VA: A. Morris, 1854. p. 241.

50. Child, *Appeal in Favor of That Class of Americans Called Africans*, p. 32.

51. Frederick Douglass, *Narrative of the Life of Frederick Douglass, An American Slave, Written by Himself.* Originally published 1845; reprinted, Mattituck, NY: Amereon House, 1988, p. 72.

52. Weld, *American Slavery As It Is*, p. 77.

53. Child, *Appeal in Favor of That Class of Americans Called Africans*, p. 44.

54. Quoted in Lowance, *Against Slavery*, p. 54.

55. Child, *Appeal in Favor of That Class of Americans Called Africans*, p. 32.

56. Quoted in Lowance, *Against Slavery*, p. 205–206.

57. Quoted in William E. Cain, ed., *William Lloyd Garrison and the Fight Against Slavery.* Boston: Bedford, 1995, p. 104.

58. Quoted in Lowance, *Against Slavery*, p. 181.

59. Quoted in Curry, *Abolitionists*, p. 93.

60. Walker, *David Walker's Appeal*, p. 43.

61. Quoted in Kelley and Lewis, *To Make Our World Anew*, p. 191.

62. Quoted in Charles Van Doren, ed., *Webster's American Biographies.* Springfield, MA: G. & C. Merriam, 1974, p. 211.

63. Johnson and Smith, *Africans in America*, p. 422.

64. Quoted in Lowance, *Against Slavery*, p. 189.

65. William Lloyd Garrison, *Thoughts on African Colonization.* Originally published 1832, reprint, New York: Arno Press, 1968, no page number available.

66. Quoted in Thomas, *Slavery Attacked*, p. 126.

67. Quoted in Philip S. Foner, ed., *Frederick Douglass: Selected Speeches and Writings.* Chicago: Lawrence Hill, 1999, p. 389.

68. Quoted in Russel B. Nye, *William Lloyd Garrison and the Humanitarian Reformers:* Boston: Little, Brown, 1955, p. 147.

69. Quoted in Kelley and Lewis, *To Make Our World Anew*, p. 214.

70. Quoted in Thomas, *Slavery Attacked*, p. 102.

71. William Ellery Channing, *The Duty of the Free States.* Boston: William Crosby, 1842, no page number available.

72. Quoted in Nye, *William Lloyd Garrison and the Humanitarian Reformers*, p. 107.

73. Quoted in Cain, *William Lloyd Garrison and the Fight Against Slavery*, p. 41.

Chapter Five: Reaction to the Movement

74. Frances Wright, *A Plan for the Gradual Abolition of Slavery in the United States.* Published 1825, no page number available.

75. Stampp, *Peculiar Institution*, p. 28.

76. Quoted in Eric McKitrick, *Slavery Defended.* Englewood Cliffs, NJ: Prentice-Hall, 1963, p. 25.

77. Child, *Appeal in Favor of That Class of Americans Called Africans*, p. 211.

78. Quoted in Lowance, *Against Slavery*, p. 176.

79. Quoted in Mayer, *All on Fire*, p. 69.

80. Quoted in Thomas, *Slavery Attacked*, p. 103.

81. William Lloyd Garrison, *The Liberator*, September 3, 1831.

82. Quoted in McKitrick, *Slavery Defended*, p. 124.

83. Quoted in Thomas, *Slavery Attacked*, pp. 53–54.

84. Quoted in Johnson and Smith, *Africans in America*, p. 367.

85. Quoted in Nye, *William Lloyd Garrison and the Humanitarian Reformers*, p. 93.

86. Quoted in Walker, *David Walker's Appeal*, p. x.

87. Quoted in Mayer, *All on Fire*, p. 124.

88. Quoted in Nye, *William Lloyd Garrison and the Humanitarian Reformers*, p. 92.

89. Quoted in Mayer, *All on Fire*, p. 200.

90. Quoted in Nye, *William Lloyd Garrison and the Humanitarian Reformers*, p. 102.

91. Quoted in Mayer, *All on Fire*, p. 217.

Chapter Six:
Distrust, Disunion, and War

92. Quoted in Mayer, *All on Fire*, p. 129.

93. Catton, *The Civil War*, p. 8.

94. George Fitzhugh, *Sociology for the South*, pp. 266–67.

95. Quoted in McKitrick, *Slavery Defended*, p. 17.

96. Quoted in Thomas, *Slavery Attacked*, p. 81.

97. Child, *Appeal in Favor of That Class of Americans Called Africans*, p. 108.

98. Quoted in Allan Nevins and Henry Steele Commager, *A Pocket History of the United States*. New York: Pocket Books, 1976, p. 207.

99. Quoted in Curry, *Abolitionists*, pp. 108–109.

100. Quoted in Johnson and Smith, *Africans in America*, p. 389.

101. Quoted in Thomas, *Slavery Attacked*, p. 130.

102. Quoted in Thomas, *Slavery Attacked*, p. 151.

103. Quoted in Nye, *William Lloyd Garrison and the Humanitarian Reformers*, p. 159.

104. Quoted in Nevins and Commager, *Pocket History of the United States*, p. 199.

105. Quoted in McKitrick, *Slavery Defended*, p. 99.

106. Quoted in Horton and Horton, *Hard Road to Freedom*, p. 163.

107. Quoted in Barnett Hollander, *Slavery in America: Its Legal History*. New York: Barnes & Noble, 1964, p. 123.

108. Quoted in Lowance, *Against Slavery*, p. 314.

109. Mayer, *All on Fire*, p. 487.

110. Quoted in Kelley and Lewis, *To Make Our World Anew*, p. 226.

111. Quoted in Catton, *Civil War*, p. 105.

112. Horton and Horton, *Hard Road to Freedom*, p. 168.

113. Quoted in Mayer, *All on Fire*, p. 547.

114. Quoted in Botkin, *Lay My Burden Down*, p. 282.

115. Quoted in Wright, New York Times *Almanac* 2005, pp. 68–69.

116. Quoted in Johnson and Smith, *Africans in America*, p. 444.

Epilogue: Afterward

117. Nevins and Commager, *Pocket History of the United States*, p. 232.

118. Child, *Appeal in Favor of That Class of Americans Called Africans*, p. 216.

For Further Reading

Books

Helaine Becker, *John Brown.* Woodbridge, CT: Blackbirch, 2001. This book deals with the abolitionist John Brown, with particular reference to his 1859 raid on the Harpers Ferry arsenal. Places Brown and his activities in historical context.

Peter Burchard, *Frederick Douglass: For the Great Family of Man.* New York: Atheneum Books for Young Readers, 2003. A well-researched biography of Frederick Douglass, one of the leaders of the abolitionist movement and a former fugitive slave.

Stephen Currie, *The Liberator: Voice of the Abolitionist Movement.* San Diego: Lucent, 2000. About William Lloyd Garrison and his antislavery newspaper; discusses Garrison's life and influences along with the effects of the newspaper on abolitionism and on social reform in general.

———, *Slavery.* Opposing Viewpoints Digests. San Diego: Greenhaven, 1999. Arguments for and against slavery, summarized and presented much as they were made shortly before the Civil War, together with an essay giving background information.

William Dudley, ed., *Slavery.* Opposing Viewpoints. San Diego: Greenhaven, 1992. A book of readings on slavery and its impact, present-ing arguments of those who attacked the institution as well as those who defended it. Though the bulk of the excerpts date from the mid-1800s, this book includes many documents from colonial and Revolutionary America as well.

Judith Edwards, *Abolitionists and Slave Resistance: Breaking the Chains of Slavery.* Berkeley Heights, NJ: Enslow, 2004. Discusses the abolitionist movement as well as how slaves escaped, rebelled, and defied their masters.

Susanne Everett, *History of Slavery.* Edison, NJ: Chartwell, 1996. A well-illustrated volume with information on slavery throughout the world and through history. Includes valuable information on slavery in the American South and the impact of the abolitionists.

Joyce Hansen, *Freedom Roads: Searching for the Underground Railroad.* Chicago: Cricket, 2002. Discusses the Underground Railroad, how it was set up and organized, and the role played by abolitionists.

Julius Lester, *To Be a Slave.* New York: Dial, 1968. A collection of slave reminiscences, together with commentary. One of the first books for young readers to describe slavery from the perspective of those enslaved.

Patricia McKissack and Fredrick L. McKissack, *Days of Jubilee: The End of Slavery in the United States.* New York: Scholastic, 2003. Describes the emancipation of American slaves and the abolition of slavery.

Tim McNeese, *The Rise and Fall of American Slavery: Freedom Denied, Freedom Gained.* Berkeley Heights, NJ: Enslow, 2004. An account of slavery as it existed in the South, with useful information about how the institution began and how the abolitionist movement helped to defeat it.

The 19th Century and Abolition. Voices in African American History. Columbus, OH: Modern Curriculum, 1994. An informative study of the abolitionists and their times.

Richard Steins, *The Nation Divides: The Civil War (1820–1880).* New York: Twenty-First Century, 1995. A description of the forces and events that led to disunion and civil war. Includes important information about the abolitionists.

Web Sites

Abolition, Anti-Slavery Movements, and the Rise of the Sectional Controversy, Library of Congress (http://memory.loc.gov/ammem/aao html/exhibit/aopart3.html). Part of the African American Odyssey exhibit. A history of the antislavery movement, told in part through documents held in the Library of Congress collections.

African-American Music, Library of Congress. (www.loc.gov/exhibits/african/afam 005.html). Another site that includes samples of documents and other antislavery works from the collection of the Library of Congress. Also includes links to other Library of Congress pages that relate to abolitionism and to black history in general.

Africans in America, WGBH Educational Foundation (www.pbs.org/wgbh/aia/part4/index .html). An index page providing links to dozens of pages about abolition, including biographical sketches of individual abolitionists, modern perspectives on the effectiveness of the movement, and many historical documents. All pages are part of the PBS Africans in America site, based on a television special.

Documents on Slavery, Avalon Project at Yale Law School (www.yale.edu/lawweb/avalon/slavery.htm). A collection of resources that relate to slavery. Many have a direct connection with the abolition movement and the people who formed it.

The Life of Frederick Douglass, National Park Service (www.nps.gov/frdo/fdlife.htm). Biographical details on this famous abolitionist, together with links to other pages of interest. This site is maintained in conjunction with the Frederick Douglass National Historic Site in Washington, D.C.

National Underground Railroad Network to Freedom, National Park Service (http://209.10.16.21/TEM PLATE/FrontEnd/index.cfm). Links and information relating to the Underground Railroad and fugitive slaves in general.

Works Consulted

Albert Barnes, *An Inquiry into the Scriptural Views of Slavery.* Philadelphia: Perkins & Purves, 1846. This book, a fine example of the kind of antislavery literature common in the 1830–1850 era, argues that the Bible does not justify slavery and that true Christians must reject the institution.

B.A. Botkin, ed., *Lay My Burden Down.* Chicago: University of Chicago Press, 1945. This is a collection of excerpts from a series of interviews with former slaves. A fascinating and moving book, it ranks among the most valuable primary sources for information on slavery from the slaves' perspectives.

William E. Cain, ed., *William Lloyd Garrison and the Fight Against Slavery.* Boston: Bedford, 1995. Excerpts from Garrison's *The Liberator* newspaper, along with clear and balanced commentary.

Allen D. Candler, *The Colonial Records of the State of Georgia: Proceedings and Minutes of the Governor and Council from Aug. 6, 1771–Feb. 13, 1782.* Atlanta: Franklin Turner, 1907. Records of meetings of the governor of Georgia during the late 18th century.

Bruce Catton, *The Civil War.* Originally published 1960. Reprint, Boston: Houghton Mifflin, 1987. One of the best one-volume histories of the Civil War. Includes a short but informative summary of the events that led to the war's outbreak.

William Ellery Channing, *The Duty of the Free States.* Boston: William Crosby, 1842. Channing was a reform-minded minister and antislavery activist who generally supported the gradualist position. This book was his great work on the subject of abolition.

Lydia Maria Child, *An Appeal in Favor of That Class of Americans Called Africans.* Originally published 1836. Reprint, New York: Arno Press, 1968. One of the most interesting of all abolitionist documents, Child's book offers a variety of antislavery arguments. Clearly written, pointedly sarcastic, and often quite compelling.

Richard O. Curry, *The Abolitionists: Reformers or Fanatics?* New York: Holt, Rinehart, and Winston, 1965. Readings taken from the works of historians who wrote on the subject of the abolitionists. The book presents a diverse set of opinions on the causes, impact, and foundations of the abolition movement.

David Brion Davis, *The Problem of Slavery in Western Culture.* Ithaca, NY: Cornell University Press, 1966. An exploration of slavery's beginnings and development in the Americas. Includes a discussion of the growth of antislavery thought in England and the British colonies before the Revolution.

Frederick Douglass, *Narrative of the Life of Frederick Douglass, An American Slave, Written by Himself.* Originally published 1845. Reprint, Mattituck, NY: Amereon House, 1988. One of several autobiographical accounts published by Douglass. Particularly useful for Douglass's experiences in slavery and his life shortly after his escape.

Stanley Feldstein, *Once a Slave: The Slave's View of Slavery.* New York: William Morrow, 1971. An overview of slavery with an emphasis on the feelings and experiences of the slaves.

George Fitzhugh, *Sociology for the South.* Richmond, VA: A. Morris, 1854. Fitzhugh was one of the most notorious defenders of slavery. This book, which presents arguments in favor of the institution, was highly influential in the South.

Philip S. Foner, ed., *Frederick Douglass: Selected Speeches and Writings.* Chicago: Lawrence Hill, 1999. A wide assortment of Douglass's works, including his views on the Constitution and much more.

William Lloyd Garrison, *The Liberator.* Garrison's abolitionist newspaper, published from 1831 through 1865.

———, *Thoughts on African Colonization.* Originally published 1832. Reprint, New York: Arno Press, 1968. An influential pamphlet expressing Garrison's opposition to the idea of sending American blacks back to Africa.

Eugene Genovese, *Roll, Jordan, Roll: The World the Slaves Made.* New York: Vintage, 1976. One of the classic books on slavery in the American South. A valuable resource for understanding the impact of the institution on the slaves themselves.

Barnett Hollander, *Slavery in America: Its Legal History.* New York: Barnes & Noble, 1964. Legal documents relating to slavery, including excerpts from the Fugitive Slave Act, the Kansas-Nebraska Act, and the Emancipation Proclamation, among many others.

James Oliver Horton and Lois E. Horton, *Hard Road to Freedom.* New Brunswick, NJ: Rutgers University Press, 2001. A history of the black experience in America.

Charles Johnson and Patricia Smith, *Africans in America.* New York: Harcourt Brace, 1998. A companion volume to a PBS television series. A good overview of slavery and its history in the United States. Also includes useful information on the abolitionist movement, particularly the role of blacks.

George Keith, *An Exhortation & Caution to Friends Concerning Buying or Keeping of Negroes.* New York: William Bradford, 1693. This pamphlet, written, printed, and distributed by Keith, is one of the very earliest antislavery writings in the British colonies. Keith's goal was to encourage his fellow Quakers not to support slavery in any way.

Robin D.G. Kelley and Earl Lewis, *To Make Our World Anew: A History of Black Americans.* New York: Oxford University Press, 2000. A thorough and well-written history of African Americans, with an emphasis on the institution of slavery and the abolitionists who fought against it.

Kate Clifford Larson, *Bound for the Promised Land.* New York: Ballantine, 2004. Biographical information about antislavery activist and Underground Railroad conductor Harriet Tubman.

Gerda Lerner, *The Grimké Sisters from South Carolina.* Chapel Hill: University of North Carolina Press, 2004. A joint biography of Angelina and Sarah Grimké, sisters who supported both abolition and women's rights despite having come from a wealthy Southern slaveholding family.

Mason Lowance, ed., *Against Slavery: An Abolitionist Reader.* New York: Penguin, 2000. A recent and informative collection of writings by the abolitionists. Focuses mainly on the period from 1830 to 1860, with a heavy emphasis on the writings of William Lloyd Garrison.

Henry Mayer, *All on Fire: William Lloyd Garrison and the Abolition of Slavery.* New York: St. Martin's, 1998. An exhaustive biography of Garrison, with valuable information on his works and his connection to the rest of the abolitionist movement.

Eric McKitrick, ed., *Slavery Defended.* Englewood Cliffs, NJ: Prentice-Hall, 1963. The proslavery arguments of Southern leaders between 1830 and the coming of the Civil War. Useful for understanding what the abolitionists were fighting against.

George H. Moore, ed., *Notes on the History of Slavery in Massachusetts.* New York: D. Appleton, 1866. Includes the text of John Saffin's proslavery tract of 1701.

Allan Nevins and Henry Steele Commager, *A Pocket History of the United States.* New York: Pocket Books, 1976. A good one-volume history of the United States.

Russel B. Nye, *William Lloyd Garrison and the Humanitarian Reformers.* Boston: Little, Brown, 1955. An early study of Garrison, with particular reference to his place within the abolitionist movement. Short but thorough and well-rounded.

Gilbert Osofsky, ed., *Puttin' on Ole Massa.* New York: Harper and Row, 1969. Three slave narratives along with commentary.

Samuel Sewall, *The Selling of Joseph: A Memorial.* Boston: Samuel Sewall,

1700. A self-published pamphlet that ranks as one of the earliest antislavery tracts in American history.

Kenneth Stampp, *The Peculiar Institution.* New York: Alfred A. Knopf, 1967. Another valuable account of slavery as it existed in the plantation South.

John L. Thomas, ed., *Slavery Attacked.* Englewood Cliffs, NJ: Prentice-Hall, 1965. A book of readings culled from the work of the abolitionists, with introductory material. This volume focuses entirely on the post–David Walker period.

Charles Van Doren, ed., *Webster's American Biographies.* Springfield, MA: G. & C. Merriam, 1974. Biographical sketches of famous Americans, including many abolitionists and political leaders of the pre–Civil War period.

David Walker, *David Walker's Appeal.* Ed. Charles M. Wiltse. Originally published 1829 under the title *Appeal to the Coloured Citizens of the World.* Reprint, New York: Hill and Wang, 1965. David Walker's furious denunciation of slavery that in some ways began the radical abolitionist movement.

Theodore Weld, *American Slavery As It Is: Testimony of a Thousand Witnesses.* Originally published 1839. Reprint, Salem, NH: Ayer, 1991. Weld's famous indictment of slavery from eyewitness reports, including excerpts from Southern newspaper advertisements and articles. Probably the single most influential book on the subject of abolition, and still compelling today.

Harvey Wish, ed., *Slavery in the South.* New York: Farrar, Straus, 1964. Nineteenth-century writings on slavery and the plantation system, from the perspectives of African Americans (both slave and free), Southern whites, and visitors to the South.

Frances Wright, *A Plan for the Gradual Abolition of Slavery in the United States.* Published 1825. A reformer with a particular interest in the emancipation of the slaves, Wright wrote this book to advocate the cause of gradual abolition.

John W. Wright, ed., The New York Times Almanac, 2005. New York: Penguin, 2005. Facts, figures, time lines, and excerpts from important documents in the history of America.

Index

Picture Credits

Cover, Hulton Archive by Getty Images
© Bettmann/CORBIS, 19, 31, 32, 55, 91
© CORBIS, 78, 87
Dover Publications, Inc., 27, 29(both), 42, 43 (both), 63
Hulton Archive by Getty Images, 14, 23, 26, 36, 41, 48 (lower), 65, 79, 88, 95
Time-Life Pictures/Getty Images, 74-75
Library of Congress, 3, 6, 10, 22, 35, 46, 48 (upper), 57, 62, 67, 68, 71, 77, 92
North Wind Picture Archive, 8, 13, 47
Steve Zmina, 11, 83

About the Author

Stephen Currie is the author of more than forty books, including a number of works on history and some historical fiction. Among his books for Lucent are *Life in a Wild West Show*, *The Olympic Games*, and *Adoption*. He is also a teacher. He grew up in Illinois and now lives with his family in upstate New York.